Max Stirner Versus Karl Marx:

Individuality and the Social Organism

Philip Breed Dematteis

STAND ALONE

VS MARX

SA1120
978-1-943687-20-6

Typeset and designed by Kevin I. Slaughter.
Transcribed from the original Dayan Weller.
Proofread by Thomas Moreland.
Cover illustration by Paigey!

Individuality And The Social Organism: The Controversy Between Max Stirner Versus Karl Marx was originally a doctoral dissertation in 1972, and later published by Revisionist Press in 1976.

This newly typeset edition is published, with kind permission of the author, by Underworld Amusements for the Union of Egoists *Stand Alone* journal.

More information at: www.UnionOfEgoists.com

2019 PREFACE

I wrote this work almost fifty years ago; I'm glad to still be alive to see this edition come out. (Actually, I'd be glad to be alive even if the edition wasn't coming out.) At that time I was quite taken with the philosophy of Max Stirner (real name: Johann Schmidt, or John Smith—just as, according to Victor Borge, Giuseppe Verdi is "Joe Green to you"). In those days I thought of myself as a conservative in politics, especially in regard to anticommunism. That's why I was fascinated to discover this little-known thinker who was a contemporary of Karl Marx and who had social and political views that were so diametrically opposed to Marx's that Marx and Friedrich Engels devoted hundreds of pages of *The German Ideology* to a refutation of him—pages that are never reprinted and are virtually forgotten, because their subject is, if known about at all, considered to be of little importance.

I suppose you could say that I actually became a Stirnerite— one of very few who ever existed, I'm sure. I already had libertarian leanings that had been instilled in me by my mother at an early age, and Stirner pushed me all the way into anarchism. I was an atheist, so we were in agreement there. And his moral nihilism--the idea that moral principles are figments of the imagination, "wheels in the head" inculcated by religion and the state, with no objective reality, was a revelation to me. I had always been unconvinced by the various ethical systems proposed by philosophers—utilitarianism, the Categorical Imperative, and so on—but I thought that there must be some objective moral standards. Stirner swept that away. On the other hand, I didn't want to be a sociopath and victimize other people, and I certainly didn't want other people to victimize me. Stirner's notion of a "union of egoists," in which each individual would look out for him- or herself and for those he or she cared about, and would expect others to do the same, seemed to solve that problem, as well as the problem of how to have a peaceful society without a government.

Well, youthful enthusiasms seldom last. From Stirner I moved on to more-sophisticated versions of libertarianism. Influenced by the writings of Murray Rothbard (whom I once met in person), I became an anarchocapitalist for a while; then Robert Nozick's *Anarchy, State and Utopia* helped to turn me into a limited-government libertarian. (Unlike many libertarians, including Rothbard, I did not come to libertarianism by way of Ayn Rand; although, as an undergraduate, long before discovering Stirner, I did write a favorable essay on her book *The Virtue of Selfishness* for a philosophy class. The professor, a leftist, gave me an "A" for my arguments while noting that he disagreed with everything Rand said.) I even went so far as to run for governor of South Carolina as a libertarian in 1978. (I lost to Dick Riley, who later became Bill Clinton's secretary of education. True story.)

I no longer call myself a libertarian, even though I still have libertarian impulses. For one thing, having pets (or maybe I should say "animal companions") has resulted in my becoming passionate about animal rights. I always found libertarians (except for Nozick, who also moved away from libertarianism, though not for that reason) weak on this point: for them, the human species was of supreme importance, and the only one with rights. I also have come to repudiate Stirner's moral nihilism: to me, cruelty to animals is just objectively wrong. I now think that the basis of morality is empathy, imagining oneself in the place of other sentient creatures. (Kind of like Jeremy Bentham's utilitarianism, but not as calculating.) Another factor pushing me away from libertarianism is the modern Republican Party, especially the Tea Party, the Freedom Caucus, and—most especially—President Donald J. Trump. I know that the argument can be made that these people are not libertarians in the strict sense (Trump, in fact, is an authoritarian demagogue), but they are too close for comfort: a lot of their rhetoric sounds like libertarianism, and they could be what libertarianism actually comes to when it acquires political power--greed, selfishness, lack of concern for the environment, and so on.

Nevertheless, I still think that Max Stirner's philosophy is worth revisiting for its uniqueness, for its lively style of presentation, and for the historical fact that it drove Marx and Engels crazy for a while. I hope that the publication of this book will play some small part in his rediscovery.

Philip Breed Dematteis
March, 2019

ACKNOWLEDGEMENTS

I am only too aware of the many shortcomings of this work, and accept full responsibility for them. I can only say in its defense that it was conceived as the first step—a very small first step—in a long-range project of study.

For whatever merits the work may possess, gratitude is due and is hereby sincerely expressed to the following friends: Professor S. Morris Eames, who directed this dissertation and provided a great deal of advice, support, and encouragement; and the members of the Committee for the Final Examination, who offered many helpful suggestions and asked many searching questions. The search for answers to some of the questions will doubtless direct my research for years to come. The members of the Committee were: Professor Lewis E. Hahn, Director of Graduate Studies of the Department of Philosophy; Professor Elizabeth R. Eames and Professor James A. Diefenbeck of the Department of Philosophy; and Professor Alan M. Cohn, of the staff of Morris Library. Special Thanks is due to Professor George Kimball Plochmann of the Department of Philosophy, my employer for the past year, for giving me time off, with pay, to complete the writing of this dissertation.

Finally, I want to thank my wife, Holly, without whose moral and material support and tireless assistance this dissertation quite literally would never have been written.

TABLE OF CONTENTS

INTRODUCTION

James Huneker relates the following incident:

> One hot August afternoon in the year 1896 at Bayreuth, I was standing in the Marktplatz when a member of the Wagner Theater pointed out to me a house opposite, at the corner of the Maximilian-strasse and said: "Do you see that house with the double gables? A man was born there whose name will be green when Jean Paul and Richard Wagner are forgotten." It was too large a draught upon my credulity, so I asked the name. "Max Stirner," he replied.[1]

Thus far, Huneker's informant has proved to be a poor prophet. The philosophy of Max Stirner has been largely ignored since its creation over one hundred years ago. One commentator asserts that "scholars are mostly content to recollect him, if they recollect him at all, by his associations, the tacit assumption being that it is only through these associations that he has any

---

1   James Huneker, *Egoists: A Book of Supermen* (1909; New York; Charles Scribner's Sons, 1932), p. 351.

historical significance or contemporary interest."[2]

Stirner has, indeed, important associations in abundance. He was a student of Hegel, the most extreme member of the school of Young Hegelians who turned their master's method against his conclusions. He then turned his dialectic against his fellow Young Hegelians and became embroiled in controversy with them; one of these was Karl Marx. His associations include membership in several other important intellectual traditions. He has been called "a key figure" in German nineteenth-century romantic individualism, "the one in a line including Goethe, Wagner, and Nietzsche who went the furthest in exploring a philosophy of the glorification of the ego in the context of political and socioeconomic ideas."[3] There is little evidence of a direct influence of Stirner upon Nietzsche, but many striking anticipations of Nietzschean ideas can be found in Stirner: "cleric"[4] and "herd"[5] morality, the "moralizing of ethically neutral words,"[6] the death of God,[7] the will to power.[8] There are also many anticipations of Freudian concepts in Stirner, among them projection and unconscious motivation,[9] libidinal repression,[10] and the egoistic character of all human acts.[11] He has also been regarded as a precursor of existentialism.[12]

When Stirner has been considered at all, however, it has

---

2   R.W.K. Paterson, *The Nihilistic Egoist: Max Stirner* (London and New York: Oxford University Press, 1971), p. vii.

3   John Carroll (ed.), *Max Stirner: The Ego and His Own* ("Roots of the Right: Readings in Fascist, Racist and Elitist Ideology"; General ed.: George Steiner; London : Jonathan Cape, 1971), p. 16.

4   *Ibid.*, pp. 196-197, n. 2.

5   *Ibid.*, p. 159 , n. 1.

6   *Ibid.*, p. 124, n. 1.

7   *Ibid.*, p. 109, n. 1.

8   *Ibid.*, p. 166, n. 1.

9   *Ibid.*, p. 253, n. 1.

10 *Ibid.*, p. 225, n. 1.

11 *Ibid.*, p. 199, n. 1.

12 Karl Löwith, *From Hegel to Nietzsche: The Revolution in Nineteenth-Century Thought*, trans. David E. Green (1941; Garden City, N. Y.: Doubleday & Company, 1967), p . 296.

usually been as an expounder of anarchism. He has been called "the father of anarchism"[13] and "the only writer to develop fully the implications of a total rejection of external authority."[14] But the very radicalism of Stirner's critique of all forms of social order has led others to deny that he is an anarchist, at least in the traditional sense.[15] Men of many political viewpoints have praised Stirner in their writings, among them Eduard Bernstein, Rudolf Steiner , and Georg Brandes.[16] He has been compared with Hobbes and Machiavelli[17] and called a precursor of Thorstein Veblen.[18]

These "associations" alone should be sufficient to show that Stirner deserves to be rescued from the intellectual oblivion into which he has fallen. Beyond this, R.W.K. Paterson contends that Stirner's is a "truly perennial"[19] and "intrinsically significant"[20] philosophy, in the sense that he is the most extreme existentialist (as he was the most extreme Young Hegelian, the most extreme romantic individualist, and the most extreme anarchist), the only one who has come to grips, without flinching, with the peculiarly modern problem of meaninglessness. Another commentator, John Carroll, sees Stirner's contemporary relevance primarily in a political context: for him, Stirner is "the first critic of liberalism as we know it today,"[7] who "unleashes one of the most savage and penetrating attacks ever written on liberal democracy."[21] He sees Stirner as a predecessor of Marcuse[22] and compares him to

---

13 George Plechanoff, *Anarchism and Socialism*, trans. Eleanor Marx Aveling (Chicago: Charles H. Kerr & Company, 1909), p. 39.

14 Carroll, *Max Stirner: The Ego and His Own*, pp. 34-35 .

15 Paterson, *The Nihilistic Egoist: Max Stirner*, pp. 138-140.

16 Carroll, *Max Stirner: The Ego and His Own*, pp. 27-28.

17 *Ibid.*, p. 121, n. 2.

18 *Ibid.*, p. 125, n. 1.

19 Paterson, *The Nihilistic Egoist: Max Stirner*, p. x.

20 *Ibid.*, p. vii.

21 *Ibid.*, p. 11.

22 *Ibid.*, p. 158 , n. l; pp. 133-134, n. 3. Cf. Eugene Fleisch-mann "The Role of the Individual in Pre-revolutionary Society: Stirner, Marx, and Hegel,"

Eldridge Cleaver and Malcolm X.[23]

Stirner's philosophy, Carroll concludes,

> gives us a philosophical framework for understand-
> ing some of the main currents of revolt in the last decade
> in the advanced industrial societies. In addition, it could
> provide at least a coherent basis for action...for a gener-
> ation disillusioned with parliamentary democracy and
> political liberalism.[24]

The present work is an attempt to reveal the intrinsic significance of Stirner's thought by considering him in relation to
the most important of his "associations": Marx. It is conceived
as the first step in a long-term project of coming to terms with
Marxism. It cannot be denied that Marxism is one of the dominant outlooks existing in the world today: not only do millions
of people live in countries governed at least ostensibly according to Marxist principles, but intellectuals in virtually all fields
of endeavor from sociology to aesthetics find in Marxism a
framework and basis for their pursuits. The reasons are not far
to seek: Marxism offers a comprehensive world-view in which
all phenomena are either explained or are held to be explainable
by a further application of its principles. In its many variations,
it provides a metaphysics, epistemology, theory of nature, ethics,
social philosophy, and politics, or at least substitutes for all of
these. In a word, it is a return to--or continuation of--the great,
all-encompassing systems which were identified with philosophy
until about the middle of the nineteenth century. Such systems
have now gone out of vogue among professional philosophers,

---

in Z. A. Pelczynski (ed.), *Hegel's Political Philosophy: Problems and Perspectives* (Cambridge: At the University Press, 1971), p. 220: "The 'great refusal' of Herbert Marcuse is clearly prefigured in Max Stirner's work, *Der Einzige und sein Eigenthum*..."

23   Carroll, *Max Stirner: The Ego and His Own*, pp. 16-17.
24   Carroll, *Max Stirner: The Ego and His Own*, pp. 30-31.

but the desire for them still seems as strong in at least some human psyches as it ever was.

The present writer is one of those attracted to this comprehensive sort of philosophy, but is at the same time repelled by the only modern version available. It seems to me, to paraphrase Fichte, that the kind of philosophy a person accepts depends ultimately upon the kind of person he is. Lewis Feuer contends that many intellectuals are attracted to Marxism because of a "latent authoritarianism" in their psychological make-up.[25] There are probably many motivations, and this may be one of them; but I believe that one factor in many cases is a temperamental preference for a holistic, collectivistic, organic view of humanity. Marxism provides an articulation of such a view as part of a comprehensive outlook, and expresses it in the irreligious, value-free, scientific terminology that is currently appealing among intellectuals. Those of us who share the desire for a comprehensive, scientific *Weltanschauung*, but have a temperamental preference for a nominalist, atomistic, individualistic view of mankind, are left with nowhere to turn.

The thought of Max Stirner offers a promise of providing an alternative to Marxism.

It springs from the same intellectual roots as does Marxism, namely, the controversies of the Young Hegelians of the mid-nineteenth century. There are many similarities of method and concepts between the two philosophies, and both are radically opposed to the prevailing social and political orders; furthermore, both lay claim to being value-free and naturalistic. In the end, however, they diverge quite markedly: Marxism is collectivistic, while Stirnerism is radically individualistic.

But Stirner as yet provides only a promise of an alternative system to that of Marx. Stirner's one philosophically important book was not a systematic treatise; but it does contain many hints and suggestions which could be elaborated into a system that

---

25 Lewis S. Feuer, *Marx and the Intellectuals: A Set of Post-Ideological Essays* (Garden City, N. Y.: Doubleday & Company, 1969), p. 59.

could compete with Marxism on the latter's own terms. Such an elaboration constitutes the long-term project referred to earlier.

The first step would seem to be to return to the scene of the actual confrontation between Stirner and Marx themselves, in order to see how their viewpoints compare when placed side by side, in their purest forms. The traditional verdict has been that the controversy was decided in Marx's favor, that Marx and Engels, in *The German Ideology*, succeeded in refuting Stirner's philosophy and laying it to rest for all time. This interpretation has been allowed to stand for three main reasons: first, Stirner was unable to reply to Marx's attack, due to the fact that it was not published during his lifetime; second, the attack itself has rarely been re-examined, but merely presumed to have been successful by those who are even aware of its existence (and when it has been considered, this has usually been done by those who share the viewpoint of its author); third, Stirner's own work has been largely forgotten, while Marxism has risen to world prominence.

The object of the present study is to re-open the controversy between Stirner and Marx in order to test the validity of this traditional verdict, The first chapter summarizes the common intellectual background of Stirner and Marx in the philosophies of Hegel and the Young Hegelians; the purpose of this discussion is to establish the basic similarity in orientation between the two men. The second chapter is an exposition of the principal points in the philosophy of Stirner. The third chapter begins with a survey of the major tenets of Marxism, then proceeds to consider the more significant of the criticisms directed by Marx against Stirner, together with the updating of those criticisms by a contemporary Marxist writer. The final chapter consists of an attempt to reply to these criticisms on Stirner's behalf, whenever possible in his own words; a brief concluding section summarizes what has been accomplished, and the significance of the accomplishment.

Sidney Hook is one of those who upholds the traditional interpretation of a Marxist victory in the dispute with Stirner. This study is undertaken in the belief that he was, nevertheless, correct when he stated that

> ...the issues which Stirner raised and Marx met...have a definite relevance to the conflict of ideas and attitudes in the contemporary world in Europe and America today. Indeed, we might even say that this is due to the fact that Stirner and Marx are here discussing the fundamental problems of any possible system of ethics or public morality.[26]

History has so far supported Hook's judgment in favor of Marx. But as Herbert Read said, "After a sleep of a hundred years the giants whom Marx thought he had slain show signs of coming to life again."[27] One reason is that Marxism has proven itself ultimately unsatisfying to many of those (including Hook himself) who were initially attracted to it. Carroll points out that:

> As a candidate for an ideology of hope and liberation, Marxism has suffered from the dated content of some of its hypotheses, the living examples of its application, and, above all, the emphasis it places on central organization and the necessary movement of largescale socio-economic forces in history. Stirner's philosophy developed from the same intellectual roots as Marxism, yet pointed to an entirely different structure of liberation.[28]

This work is a small step in the attempt to define that different structure of liberation, to find other answers to those

---

26 Sidney Hook, *From Hegel to Marx: Studies in the Intellectual Development of Karl Marx* (1936; Ann Arbor: The University of Michigan Press, 1968), p. 165.

27 Herbert Read, *The Tenth Muse: Essays in Criticism* (London: Routledge and Kegan Paul, 1957), p. 75.

28 Carroll, *Max Stirner: The Ego and His Own*, p. 30.

fundamental problems of ethics and public morality, and, in advancement of those ends, to assist in the re-awakening of Max Stirner.

Chapter I

THE HEGELIAN
BACKGROUND

The thought of Hegel was the matrix in which the philosophies of Stirner and Marx took shape. Each was to react against this common birthright in different ways; yet the system of Hegel is so rich and all-embracing, and, perhaps as a consequence, so ambiguous in its ultimate import, that virtually every element of the philosophies of Stirner and Marx can be traced back to it. Despite their intentions and their assessments of their achievements, neither succeeded in completely breaking away from the position of their master. Rather, each developed different strains of his thought, thereby making manifest what was latent in Hegelianism all along.

Stirner attended Hegel's lectures at the University of Berlin from 1826 to 1828. When Marx arrived in 1837, Hegel had been dead for six years; but the university was "still under the domination of Hegel's philosophy."[29] Marx attended the lectures of Hegel's disciple, Gans, who noted his "excellent diligence" in the course.[30] While vacationing in the country, Marx became

---

29 David McLellan, *The Thought of Karl Marx: An Introduction* (London: Macmillan, 1971), pp. 3-4.

30 Franz Mehring, *Karl Marx: The Story of His Life* trans. Edward Fitzgerald;

a member of a "Doctors' Club" of Hegelians, and through this group he became "more and more chained" to the Hegelian philosophy.[31] In addition to these personal contacts, both men had access to those of Hegel's works which were published during their lifetimes; neither was familiar with Hegel's youthful writings or with his earlier formulations of his system (the "Jenenser system"), all of which are useful for the interpretation of his mature thought.[32]

Hegel had many followers, all working out their own variations of Hegelianism: some saw themselves as preserving Hegel's teachings, while others conceived their work as a reinterpretation or even a transformation of Hegel's thought. Stirner and Marx allied themselves with the latter group, the "Left" or "Young" Hegelians, and their interpretations of Hegel were based upon, and extended, the achievements of this group.

In this chapter I shall try to place Stirner and Marx in their intellectual context by discussing first the philosophy of Hegel, and then the split among Hegel's students, with special attention to the Young Hegelians.

1. Hegel

It is extremely difficult to present an exposition of Hegel's philosophy, particularly within a brief compass. Hegel's thought is so rich, deep, vast, and subtle that it virtually oversteps the bounds of language, and is expressed in a style and terminology that one of his translators calls "abstruse linguistic chaos".[33] Commentators

---

ed. Ruth and Heinz Norden (New York: Covici, Friede, 1935), p. 38

31 Lloyd D. Easton and Kurt H. Guddat (eds. And trans.), *Writings of the Young Marx on Philosophy & Society* (Garden City, N.Y.: Doubleday & Company, 1967), p. 48.

32 For the publishing history of Hegel's works, see the Bibliographical Note in Georg Wilhelm Friedrich Hegel, *Early Theological Writings*, trans. T. M. Knox and Richard Kroner {Chicago: The University of Chicago Press, 1948) , pp. 331-332.

33 Gustav Emil Mueller (trans.), *Hegel: Encyclopedia of Philosophy* (New

Max Stirner Versus Karl Marx

are left with the options of reproducing his language, and thereby failing to advance comprehension, or translating it into plainer terms, and so risk falsifying his thought.

In the few pages available here, I shall try to present my own general impression of Hegel, touching only upon such details as necessary to show his influence on Stirner and Marx. This is not to say that either Stirner or Marx consciously adopted the interpretation to be given here; no doubt each had his own interpretation of Hegel, different from each other and from what Hegel intended. This would not be surprising, since, it has been said, the interpreters of Hegel have contradicted each other almost as much as the commentators on the Bible.[34] The reason, again, is the richness and comprehensiveness of Hegel's thought. He tried to encompass all reality in his system; it is a measure of his success that his system, like reality itself, bears many possibilities within it. Almost any question about Hegel can be answered in opposite ways: he has been regarded as a theist and an atheist (and a pantheist), a totalitarian and a democrat, a nationalist and an anti-nationalist, a believer in freedom and in determinism; some feel that he thought his own time and philosophy were final, others that he left room for future development. All of these positions can be found in his system, some stated literally, some metaphorically, some merely implied. Anyone who tries to make sense of Hegel must select out some of these strains as the most important, and explain away the rest.

Stirner and Marx were lifelong Hegelians, and each developed certain of the strains of Hegel's thought farther than had Hegel himself. Therefore, their disputes with Hegel and their controversy with each other can almost be seen as disputes of Hegel with himself.

My reading of Hegel is broad enough to include the positions of both Stirner and Marx. This reading may have been

York: Philosophical Library, 1959), p. 1.

34   Jacob Loewenberg (ed.), *Hegel: Selections* (New York: Charles Scribner's Sons, 1929), p. xii.

achieved by looking at Hegel through these later philosophies, thereby reading something into Hegel that is not really there; I believe rather that the later philosophies enable us more clearly to discern what was there all the time. This contention will have to be supported by the exposition itself.

The exposition will be divided into two parts: first, Hegel's conception of dialectic; second, a brief summary of his system, emphasizing those points which seem especially relevant to the later development of Stirner and Marx.

2. The Dialectic

The dialectic is central to Hegel's philosophy; it might not overstate the case to say that it *is* his philosophy. He seems to regard the dialectic as his most important philosophical discovery, the one which forms the basis of the rest of his achievements. Furthermore, an understanding of what Hegel meant by the dialectic seems to illuminate hitherto obscure aspects of his system. This, then, seems to be the proper place to begin an exposition of Hegel, rather than his notion of Spirit.

I shall deal with the dialectic from two standpoints: first, its ontological status--what it is; second, its form--how it works.

3. Ontological Status of the Dialectic

The point of fundamental importance about the dialectic is that its nature is twofold: it is both a method of philosophy and an aspect of reality. Hegel stresses this identity of method and reality many times. For example, he says:

> I could not of course imagine that the Method which in this System of Logic I have followed--or rather which this System follows of itself--is not capable of much improvement, of much elaboration in detail, but at the same time I know that it is the only true Method. This is

already evident from the fact that the Method is no ways different from its object and content;--for it is the content in itself, *the Dialectic which it has in itself*, that moves it on. It is clear that no expositions can be regarded as scientific which do not follow the course of this Method, and which are not conformable to its simple rhythm, for that is the course of the thing itself.[35]

The following comment is also representative:

Dialectic, the logic of philosophy, is the explication (Ur-Teil) of the Concept in all essential shapes of life, in nature, soul, mind, and spirit. The movement of these living contents and the movement of dialectical thought is one and the same.[36]

Hegel sometimes refers to the dialectical process of reality as the "form" of reality, and defines philosophical method as "the consciousness of the form taken by the inner spontaneous movement of the content."[37] But since the process of reality is identical with the method, he at times calls the method itself the form: "What we have to do with here is philosophical *science* and in such science content is essentially bound up with form."[38]

Other interpreters agree that Hegel is to be taken at his word on this identity between method and reality. Marcuse says: "The philosophical method he elaborated was intended to reflect the actual process of reality and to construe it in an adequate form."[39]

---

35 W. H. Johnston and L. G. Struthers (trans.), *Hegel's Science of Logic* (1929; 2 Vols.; London: George Allen & Unwin; New York: Macmillan Company, 1951), I, 65.

36 Mueller, *Hegel: Encyclopedia of Philosophy*, sec. 474, p. 286.

37 Johnston and Struthers, *Hegel's Science of Logic*, I, 64.

38 T. M. Knox (trans.), *Hegel's Philosophy of Right* (1952; London, Oxford, and NewYork: Oxford University Press, 1969), p. 2.

39 Herbert Marcuse, *Reason and Revolution: Hegel and the Rise of Social Theory* (2d ed.; New York: Humanities Press, 1954), p. 122.

According to Dupré, "Dialectic is more than just one philosophical method among others; it is at once the self-development of thought and of reality."[40] And Findlay says:

> Hegel has no merely subjective, no merely linguistic or conceptual view of the contradictions involved in dialectic. He does not limit contradictions to misapplied or misguided notions or principles; he goes further, and attributes them to "the world."... Such Dialectic is manifest in the motions of the heavenly bodies, in political revolutions from anarchy to despotism, and in the paradoxical shifts and switches of emotional mood and expression.[41]

The revolutionary character of Hegel's identification of the dialectical method in philosophy with the movement of reality may be clarified by contrasting it with the original conception of dialectic as held by the Greeks. Hegel recognizes a kinship between his own dialectic and those of Plato and Socrates:

> Besides, dialectic in philosophy is nothing new. Among the ancients, Plato was called the discoverer of dialectic, and justly so, insofar as in the Platonic philosophy the dialectic appeared for the first time in free and therewith also objective form. In Socrates the dialectic still had, in conformity with the general character of his philosophizing, a predominantly subjective shape, namely that of irony.[42]

---

40   Louis Dupré, *The Philosophical Foundations of Marxism* (New York: Harcourt, Brace & World, 1966), p. 43.

41   J. N. Findlay, *Hegel: A Re-examination* (1958; New York: Collier Books, 1962), p. 62.

42   Georg Wilhelm Friedrich Hegel, *Werke in zwanzig Bänden* (Frankfurt am Main:Suhrkamp Verlag, 1971), VIII, 173-174. My translation.

The dialectical method is usually thought of as having originated with the Eleatics, particularly Zeno,[43] and developed as a principal method by Plato and as a secondary method by Aristotle. The significant difference between the Greek and the Hegelian conceptions of dialectic is that for the Greeks, dialectic is a mental process only: it is the process whereby the mind endeavors to adequate itself to reality. But the reality which is the goal of philosophical cognition is a static one: it is the One of the Eleatics, the Forms of Plato, or the first principles and essences of Aristotle. Insofar as "reality" is in flux, it is either illusion or a reality of an inferior grade. The dialectic is an instrument which is required only because of the weakness of the human mind; when the mind arrives at its destination of knowledge, the process ceases and the mind, like its objects, is at rest.

For Hegel, on the contrary, the process within the mind is a duplication of a process taking place in reality itself; it is, in fact, a continuation of this very process. The mind does not "cut through" the flux of appearance to an immutable reality "behind" it; reality *is* the changing appearance.[44]

Hegel feels that since the time of the Greeks, dialectic has come to be "regarded as an isolated part of Logic,"[45] as a negative and skeptical rather than a positive method. Kant's achievement, in the "Transcendental Dialectic," was to show that this negativity was inherent in reason, and not an arbitrary procedure.[46] But the cleavage between thought and reality was maintained in Kant: ultimate reality, the "thing-in-itself," was held to be inaccessible to theoretical reason. Thus the fact that dialectic was a necessary mental operation left open the question whether an identical process occurred in reality, and indicated that it did

---

43 Milton C. Nahm, *Selections from Early Greek Philosophy* (4th ed.; New York: Appleton-Century-Crofts, 1964), p . 78.

44 Cf. Michael Beresford Foster, *The Political Philosophies of Plato and Hegel* (1935; New York: Russell & Russell, 1965), pp. 121-123.

45 Johnston and Struthers, *Hegel's Science of Logic*, I, 66.

46 *Ibid.*

not. Hegel, following Schelling,[47] eliminates the thing-in-itself, thereby uniting subject and object. It follows that if dialectic is a necessary process of the mind, it is also a process of the reality cognized by that mind.

Hegel's remark that "the truth is the whole"[48] suggests a coherence theory of truth, but it seems that he actually holds to a very radical correspondence theory: not only do the "ideas" somehow "match up" with objects, but the very process of reasoning is in harmony with the flux of reality.

Hegel is saying that if reality is to be cognizable by mind, it must have certain features in common with mind: like knows like. But his contention is more thoroughgoing than this: he maintains that mind and reality are, ultimately, identical: "All opposites in reality are also opposites in philosophical reflection. Reality is in thought, thought is in reality."[49] Again, he says: "In my view...everything depends on grasping and expressing the ultimate truth not as Substance but as Subject as well."[50] And again: "If...the Idea passes for 'only an idea', for something represented in an opinion, philosophy rejects such a view and shows that nothing is actual except the Idea."[51]

The human mind is not something set over against or opposed to reality, but a part of the real and continuous with it, so that in knowing reality the mind is actually knowing its own larger self. This universal, mental reality, which encompasses both the mind and the material universe, Hegel calls Spirit (*Geist*):

> That the truth is only realized in the form of system, that substance is essentially subject, is expressed in the

---

47 *Ibid.*, Georg Wilhelm Friedrich Hegel, *The Phenomenology of Mind*, trans. J. B. Bailie (1931; 2d ed.; New York: The Humanities Press, 1964), p. 80.

48 Hegel, *The Phenomenology of Mind*, p. 81.

49 Mueller, *Hegel: Encyclopedia of Philosophy*, sec. 37, p. 96.

50 Hegel, *The Phenomenology of Mind*, p. 80.

51 Knox, *Hegel's Philosophy of Right*, p. 10.

idea which represents the Absolute as Spirit (*Geist*)--the grandest conception of all, and one which is due to modern times and its religion. Spirit is alone reality. It is the inner being of the world, that which essentially is, and is *per se*; it assumes objective, determinate form, and enters into relations with itself--it is externality (otherness), and exists for self; yet, in this determination, and in its otherness, it is still one with itself--it is self-contained and self-complete, in itself and for itself at once.[52]

In Hegel's monistic view of reality, as in Spinoza's, there are no great cleavages or sharp breaks in the universe, as between God and nature, mind and matter, freedom and determinism, soul and body.[53] But Spinoza, in his unification of mind and nature, has reduced mind to the mechanical, deterministic level of nature; Hegel criticizes Spinoza's unification of reality into "One Substance" in which "self- consciousness was simply submerged, and not preserved."[54] Hegel's own approach has more in common with that of Whitehead's "philosophy of organism":[55] the lower levels of reality are to be understood on analogy with the higher,[56] not, as in Spinoza, in the reverse fashion.

Because of his identification of reality with mind, Hegel's philosophy is typically considered a form of idealism. But Hegel denies this as a proper characterization of his position:

---

52 Hegel, *The Phenomenology of Mind*, p. 85-86.

53 Cf. Harry Austryn Wolfson, *The Philosophy of Spinoza* (1934; 2 Vols. in one; New York: The World Publishing Company, 1965), II, 333-336.

54 Hegel, *The Phenomenology of Mind*, p. 80.

55 Alfred North Whitehead, *Process and Reality: An Essay in Cosmology* (1929; New York: Harper & Row, 1960). For Whitehead, even the most basic constituents of reality, the actual entities, perform rudimentary analogues of the mental activities of feeling and perception (pp. 28-29) . Oddly, Whitehead recognizes a kinship to Spinoza (p. 10), but only an indirect one, through Bradley, to Hegel. Hegel is mentioned only once, in a list of great philosophers (p. 16).

56 Mueller, *Hegel: Encyclopedia of Philosophy*, sec. 192, p. 165.

It is not an idealism in which the content of knowledge is through and through subjective, imprisoning its products within the subject; subject and object are only distinct, but necessary, poles within comprehensive, universal concreteness. The contrast of idealistic and realistic philosophy is of no importance; such expressions as subjectivity and objectivity, reality and identity, are simply bare abstractions.[57]

Mueller agrees that Hegel's "'absolute idealism' might just as well be called 'absolute realism,' but is neither, because any standpoint which has an opposite is not the Absolute."[58] It is nevertheless true that Hegel's monism is an assimilation of the non-mental to the mental, not the reverse; the ultimate reality is *Geist* not *Natur*. But paradoxically, this position opens the way for the later materialistic philosophies of Feuerbach, Stirner, and Marx, as Avineri points out:

Once Hegel has solved the problem implicit in the tension between matter and spirit by postulating matter as one of spirit's manifestations, albeit an inferior one, the traditional dualism of Western philosophy was overcome, and Hegel was of course the first to point this out. But once the spiritual substance of matter was recognized, i.e. once matter was shown to be nothing but spirit in self-alienation, then, paradoxically, matter was also rehabilitated in a fashion far more far-reaching than anything hitherto known to Western philosophy. Even eighteenth-century French materialism could not have achieved anything like it. From Hegel on, matter could no longer be conceived as the absolute negation of spirit or as its total absence.[59]

---

57 *Ibid.*, sec. 5, p. 71.
58 *Ibid.*, note.
59 Shlomo Avineri, *The Social and Political of Karl Marx* (Cambridge: At

On occasion Hegel identifies reality not merely with mind in a broad sense, but with reason: "*What is rational is actual and what is actual is rational.*"[60] On its face, this statement seems to justify whatever exists as rational and, therefore, as good; it appears to be one of the most quietistic, conservative statements ever uttered. Interpreters have sought to rescue Hegel from this implication by pointing out that Hegel identifies with the rational, not the "real" (*real*), but the "actual" (*wirklich*). "Real" denotes mere existence, while "actual" is reserved for those things which fully live up to their definitions,[61] which do not fall short of, but fully realize, their own natures,[62] or in which "the discrepancy between the possible and the real has been overcome."[63] Thus "real" is merely factual, while "actual" has honorific connotations.

This interpretation, however, runs aground on another of Hegel's statements: "To comprehend what is, this is the task of philosophy, because what is, is reason" ("...*das was ist*, ist die Vernunft").[64] Here there can be no confusion between "real" and "actual"; Hegel says that what exists is not just reasonable, but reason itself.

Hegel conceives of reality on the model of the human mind, and the latter is, in its essence, reason; therefore, reality is basically reason. But not even the human mind exerts its full rational capacity at all times; it usually operates at the lower level of understanding (*Verstand*) and often at lower levels still, in what we ordinarily describe as "irrational" behavior. The core of the mind, even here, is still reason, but it is now "surrounded" by irrationality. Similarly, "external" reality is, at bottom, rational, but manifests itself for the most part in the forms of irrationality,

---

the University Press, 1968), p. 6.

60   Knox, *Hegel's Philosophy of Right*, p. 10.

61   *Ibid.*, p. 302, no. 27.

62   Walter Kaufmann, "The Hegel Myth and Its Method," in Walter Kaufmann (ed.), *Hegel's Political Philosophy* (New York: Atherton Press, 1970), p. 152.

63   Marcuse, *Reason and Revolution*, p. 153.

64   Knox, *Hegel's Philosophy of Right*, p. 11.; Hegel, *Werke*, VII, 26.

transiency, and contingency. Hegel characterizes the situation in picturesque terms:

> For since rationality...enters upon external existence simultaneously with its actualization, it emerges with an infinite wealth of forms, shapes, and appearances. Around its heart it throws a motley covering with which consciousness is at home to begin with, a covering which the concept has first to penetrate before it can find the inward pulse and feel it still beating in the outward appearances. But the infinite variety of circumstance which is developed in this externality by the light of the essence glinting in it--this endless material and its organization--this is not the subject matter of philosophy.[65]

In fact, the only place where reason shows itself in its fully developed form as reason is in the thought of the philosopher, when he is doing philosophy. Reality is a hierarchy with the philosopher, when thinking philosophically, at the top, and man's other activities and institutions, and finally, nature, constituting lower, less fully rational levels.[66] But a rational core can be disentangled from the variety of appearances which exist on the lower levels, and it is the task of philosophy to do this. Philosophy is a vindication of what exists as rational, not in all its details, but at its center. The goal of this activity is to liberate the philosopher from and elevate him above these details, "without denying their irrational reality."[67]

4 . The Process of Dialectic

Our conception of the process of dialectic must be kept rather

---

65   Knox, *Hegel's Philosophy of Right*, p. 10-11

66   Cf. Frithjof Bergmann, "The Purpose of Hegel's System," *Journal of the History of Philosophy*, Vol. II, No. 2 (1964), 204.

67   Mueller, *Hegel: Encyclopedia of Philosophy*, sec. 5, p. 70-71.

loose. It does not seem to be the rigorous, deductive method it has traditionally been interpreted as being;[68] in particular, the tight, rigid schematism of thesis-antithesis-synthesis seems too confining. Kaufmann states that Hegel "never once used these three terms together to designate three stages in an argument or account," and that the one place he does use them is where he "roundly reproaches Kant for having 'everywhere posited thesis, antithesis, synthesis.'"[69] Kaufmann goes on to show that the structures of several of Hegel's most important works are not analyzable in terms of thesis, antithesis, and synthesis.[70]

Kaufmann and Mueller[71] contend that the thesis-antithesis-synthesis "legend" arose from Hegel's practice of dividing his writings into sections, usually in groups of three, and giving each section a number, letter, and title. A glance at these headings gives the impression of a triadic progression; these section titles are frequently reproduced in the form of charts which presume to give a synopsis of this development from thesis to antithesis to synthesis.[72] But these writers claim that the divisions were afterthoughts on Hegel's part, introduced to organize his overabundant material. Hegel's own comment supports this contention:

> In accordance with this Method I would observe that the divisions and headings of the Books, Sections, and Chapters which are given in the work, as well as to some extent the explanations connected with them, were made for the purposes of a preliminary survey, and that in fact

---

68   E.g., J. M . E . McTaggart, *Studies in the Hegelian Dialectic* (New York: Cambridge University Press, 1896), pp. 101- 102 ; W . T. Stace, *The Philosophy of Hegel* (1924 ; New York: Dover, 1955), p. 54.

69   Walter Kaufmann, *Hegel: Reinterpretation, Texts, and Commentary* (Garden City, N.Y.: Doubleday & Company, 1965), p. 168.

70   *Ibid.*, pp. 168-170, 198, 208, 212-213, 284-285.

71   Gustav Emil Mueller, "The Hegel Legend of Thesis-Antithesis-Synthesis," *Journal of the History of Ideas*, Vol. XIX, No. 3 (June 1958), 411-414.

72   E.g., Johnston and Struthers, *Hegel's Science of Logic*, I, between pp. 24-25; Findlay, *Hegel: A Re-examination*, pp. 361-373.

they have only a *historical* value. They do not belong to the content and body of the Science, but are compiled by external reflection...[73]

While the movement of thought and reality is freer than this iron law of thesis-antithesis-synthesis would indicate, the traditional pattern was not, I believe, simply imposed upon Hegel's thought from a too-hasty perusal of his tables of contents; it does express, though in an overly rigid and abstract way, the actual process.

The process can be most simply characterized by the terms "unification" and "opposition"; but as these terms are themselves in opposition, the latter is probably basic. Hegel was concerned from his youth with the problem of reconciliation of opposites. In his youthful theological writings, for example, he deals with the opposition between the formal, rational demands of the Kantian ethics, and the spontaneous, customary morality of the Greeks, and tries to construct a fusion of the two.[74] In "The Constitution of Germany," he calls for the unification of the feudal German principalities into a centralized power.[75]

The dialectic is his mature solution to this problem. It is a continual process of opposition, resulting in a unification, which again is subject to opposition, and so on. The triadic nature of this process is evident; thus the thesis-antithesis-synthesis formula has some justification. According to Marcuse, Hegel first claims that the triad (*Triplizität*) is the true form of thought in an early (1800-1802) article, "Faith and Knowledge,"[76] where "he does not state it as an empty schema of thesis, antithesis, and synthesis, but as the dynamic unity of opposites. It is the proper form of thought because it is the proper form of a reality in which

---

73 Johnston and Struthers, *Hegel's Science of Logic*, I, 65.
74 Hegel, *Early Theological Writings*.
75 T. Knox (trans.), *Hegel's Political Writings* (Oxford: At the Clarendon Press, 1964), pp. 143-242.
76 Hegel, *Werke*, II, 287-392.

Max Stirner Versus Karl Marx

every being is the synthetic unity of antagonistic conditions."[77]

In the first edition of his encyclopedia, Hegel gives this concise account of the nature of dialectic:

> There are three aspects in every thought which is logically real or true: The abstract or rational form, which says what something is; the dialectical negation, which says what something is not; the speculative-concrete comprehension: *A* is also that which it is not, *A* is non-*A*. These three aspects do not constitute three parts of logic, but are moments of everything that is logically real or true. They belong to every philosophical Concept. Every Concept is rational, is abstractly opposed to another, and is united in comprehension together with its opposites. *This is the definition of dialectic.*[78]

For Hegel, then, the world is a tense unification of opposites; each entity is what it is and also what it is not. The definition of anything, when fully understood, is seen to include the opposite of the thing: a desk is only a desk insofar as it is *not* a non-desk; a man is a master only insofar as he has a slave . The full reality of the thing includes its opposite; as soon as it is posited, so is its opposite. If the characteristics of the thing are developed to their highest degree, the thing *becomes* its opposite, since it has at the same time been developing the characteristics of its opposite.

In the *Logic*, Hegel exhibits this dialectical process in its most general form. As usual, the convoluted Hegelian jargon tends to obscure what is happening. The categories seem to be "generating" or "passing over into" each other.[79] It is difficult to understand what this could mean. Marcuse seems to state the situation more clearly:

---

77 Marcuse, *Reason and Revolution*, p. 156.
78 Mueller, *Hegel: Encyclopedia of Philosophy*, sec. 13, p. 82.
79 Findlay, Hegel: A Re-examination, p. 156.

It is not quite correct to say that one category "passes into" another. The dialectical analysis rather reveals one category as another, so that the other represents its unfolded content—unfolded by the contradictions inherent in it .[80]

On the side of the mind contemplating the categories, the full comprehension of what a category involves reveals that it includes or implies its opposite; and so the dialectical movement is that of the human mind, which is led from the contemplation of one category to the contemplation of its contrary. This is the dialectic as method. But the dialectical process also occurs in reality, where the *things* from which the categories are abstracted actually do change into one another . For example, the first two categories in the *Logic* are Being and Nothing. Pure Being is being considered in abstraction from all determinations that would render it a particular kind of being; but the absence of all determination is the distinguishing mark of non-being, or Nothing. Thus the category of Being is ultimately identical with the category of Nothing; the mind considering the first category is led to the second, which is its negation.[81] As applied to reality, these categories show that all things are at the same time being and nothing , insofar as they are temporal and contingent: each thing is continually in process of transition from being to nothing, from existence to destruction.

These are the first two "moments" of the dialectical process: as soon as a thing comes into existence, it calls up or implies its opposite, which is "foreign" or "alien" (fremb) to it. This is the basic source in the dialectic of the concept of alienation,[82] which has many concrete manifestations in Hegel's system and is of fundamental importance for Stirner and Marx.

The third moment of the process is in a sense a repetition

---

80 Marcuse, *Reason and Revolution*, p. 131.
81 Johnston and Struthers, *Hegel's Science of Logic*, I, 94.
82 Dupré, *The Philosophical Foundations of Marxism*, p. 81.

of the second: it is another negation, a "negation of negation" (*Negation der Negation*).[83] The first two moments are cancelled, but at the same time preserved; and through this cancelling and preserving they are

raised to a higher, more inclusive level, at which they find their true unification. In the *Logic*, for example, the first two categories, Being and Nothing, are negated and united in the third category, Becoming.[84] The word which expresses these three meanings of cancelling, preserving, and raising (literally, "lifting up") is *aufheben*. Hegel recognizes that this word, with its diametrically opposed meanings, is peculiar to German; he believes that its possession of such words is one of German's "many advantages over other modern language" and "reveals a speculative spirit in the language."[85]

As a mental process or method, dialectic takes the form of seeing that this aspect implies its opposite; then taking a broader view and realizing that the actual situation includes both sides in a tense harmony. This seems to be what Hegel has in mind when he calls philosophy "the liberation of the spirit from the insufficiency and one-sidedness of all forms of life; in passing beyond them, they are nevertheless preserved and ultimately grounded."[86] As a process in reality, it is exemplified in the growth of a plant, where each stage- seed, sprout, flower, etc. -reaches its optimum development only to be negated and replaced by the next;[87] or in the succession of nations, empires, and peoples, rising and declining, in political history. Hegel characterizes his *Phenomenology* as depicting such a dialectical process:

In the *Phenomenology of Spirit* I have set out an example

---

83   Johnston and Struthers, *Hegel's Science of Logic*, I, 127; Hegel, *Werke*, V, 123.

84   Johnston and Struthers, *Hegel's Science of Logic*, I, 95; Hegel, *Werke*, V, 83.

85   Johnston and Struthers, *Hegel's Science of Logic*, I, 40.

86   Mueller, *Hegel: Encyclopedia of Philosophy*, sec. 13, p. 82.

87   Knox, *Hegel's Philosophy of Right*, p. ix.

of this Method as applied to a more concrete object, namely to Consciousness [footnote: "And later as applied to other concrete objects, and corresponding departments of Philosophy"]. We have here modes of consciousness each of which in realizing itself abolishes itself, has its own negation as its result, -and thus passes over into a higher mode.[88]

There is another exemplification of the dialectical process of reality which is formulated by some Marxists as a separate "law" of the dialectic: the transformation of quantity into quality. In the *Logic*, Hegel discusses these two categories and shows that when a given quantity is developed to a high enough degree- that is, increased to a certain point- it becomes a change in quality. Applying this to reality, Hegel concludes that natural processes are not continuous, but proceed in quantum leaps; for example:

> Water on being cooled does not little by little become hard, gradually reaching the consistency of a paste, but is suddenly hard; when it already has quite attained freezing-point it may (if it stands still) be wholly liquid, and a slight shake brings it into the condition of hardness.[89]

Marcuse sums up this "law": "There is no even progress in the world; the appearance of every new condition involves a leap; the birth of the new is the death of the old."[90] This should be qualified: the old is never totally annihilated , but is preserved and transformed in the next stage: thus the fruit of the plant does not come into existence *ex nihilo*, but retains the progress in complexity that the flower has attained as compared with the root, and so on.

In summary, Hegel's vision of reality is one of a constant

---

88 Johnston and Struthers, *Hegel's Science of Logic*, I, 64.
89 *Ibid.*, I, 389-390.
90 Marcuse, *Reason and Revolution*, p. 141.

interplay of oppositions, which achieve a tense harmony and constitute a single universe. The dialectic is the formulation, in abstract terms, of this process. It is not a method to be imposed arbitrarily upon whatever subject is being investigated, and it does not result in deductive certainty; rather , it is a way of looking at the world, of having a "feeling" for the oppositions, conflicts, disharmonies, and paradoxes upon which the world moves. Hegel bequeathed this outlook to Stirner and Marx, both of whom, in different ways, made it central to their philosophies.

5. The System

One section of one chapter is obviously much too short to allow even a synopsis of Hegel's entire system. The discussion will have to be restricted to the barest mention of those aspects which are important for the later development of Stirner and Marx.

Hegel is a philosopher who takes seriously the task of comprehending reality, a task which is ultimately identical with that of comprehending human thought: reality is spirit, which reaches its highest development in the human mind. In reflecting upon itself, the mind is comprehending reality:

> As Concept (*Begriff*), reality becomes conscious of itself in the thinking mind. Herein philosophy seems to be occupied exclusively with the thinking mind and sundered from the richness of the sensuous world; and from the more concrete and intelligible historical world. But the dialectic of philosophy is not confined to the actual subject: It pertains equally to the structures of Being, to essential universals . Philosophy, in this enlarged sense, is cognition of reality as such. [91]

A problem arises here: if there is a God in Hegel's system, it

---

91 Johnston and Struthers, *Hegel's Science of Logic*, I, 39.

would seem that he, and not man, would be the supreme manifestation of Spirit; and Hegel does frequently talk about God. He says, for example, that the content of logic "shows forth God as he is in his eternal essence before the creation of Nature and of a finite Spirit,"[92] and that world history "is the true Theodicaea, the justification of God in History."[93] In spite of such statements, however, some commentators contend that Hegel was not a theist,[94] and the present writer agrees with this position. As usual, Hegel also makes statements which tend in the other direction. This ambiguity was one of the sources of the split among his followers.

Hegel's non-theistic statements, however, appear to be broad enough to explain the theistic ones . He places religion, along with philosophy and art, in the sphere of "absolute Spirit," and says that they all have the same content, but express it in different ways.[95] They are three ways of grasping reality as a spiritual, developing oppositional unity. Art expresses this reality in the form of sensuous intuition, religion in the form of myth and symbol. But philosophy grasps and expresses the whole in purely rational form, and this form, being more akin to reality itself, is the most adequate. Therefore, philosophy transcends and includes the other two disciplines.[96] On the relation between philosophy and religion, and the use of religious terminology in philosophy, Hegel says:

> *Philosophy* thus understands religion as one of its own presuppositions and as a particular articulation of the absolute totality. It sees through the form of mythical representations by virtue of which the life of the absolute

---

92 *Ibid.*, I, 60.

93 Georg Wilhelm Friedrich Hegel, *The Philosophy of History*, trans. J. Sibree (1899; New York: Dover Publications, 1956), p. 457.

94 E.g., Findlay, *Hegel: A Re-examination*, pp. 142-143.

95 Mueller, *Hegel: The Encyclopedia of Philosophy*, sec. 473, p. 285.

96 *Ibid.*, sec. 472, p. 282.

is pictured in seemingly discreet stories, quasi-temporal myths, and cultic symbols.

Philosophy uses such language without being taken captive by it. The revelation of the Absolute is not confined to religion, but can and must be thought in the logical form of truth.[97]

Hegel's "God," then, knows himself in man's knowledge of the universe. This is not to say that man is God: "The metaphysical lie and radical evil in this: a finite will pretends to play God."[98] Man is an aspect of "God", but "God" is nothing less than the totality of the real: "God is...that absolute whole which has nothing alien outside of itself...."[99]

Hegel's "God," like Spinoza's, is the absolute totality of being, of which man is a self-conscious part. But Spinoza's God is timeless; we perceive change over time because of our finite perspective. If we rise to the level of the "intellectual love of God," we will see everything *sub specie aeternitatis*. For Hegel, on the other hand, reality, as spirit, is in flux, always changing dialectically. The Absolute is really a series of relative Absolutes; at each stage of its development, some men can comprehend it in art, religion, and philosophy, and to a lesser degree in other disciplines such as natural science. The development of knowledge over the centuries is not a progress toward some goal where it will finally be able to come to rest; the object of knowledge is in itself changing, and knowledge must change along with it. But man's knowledge will become deeper, fuller, and richer, because the Absolute itself is becoming so: "The present form of Spirit comprehends within it all earlier steps."[100]

The task of philosophy is to comprehend reality as it exists at the present time: "Philosophy...is its own time apprehended

---

97 *Ibid.*, sec. 471, pp. 283-284.
98 *Ibid.*, sec. 469, p. 282.
99 *Ibid.*, p. 278.
100 Hegel, The *Philosophy of History*, p. 79.

in thoughts."[101] It gathers up the present spiritual achievements of mankind, which are partial manifestations of reality, and integrates them into a system in which the rational structure of the real will be evident. Philosophy does not criticize the actual in comparison to some transcendent, timeless norm;[102] "Even Plato's *Republic* which passes proverbially as an empty ideal, is in essence nothing but an interpretation of the nature of Greek ethical life."[103] A similar deprecation of criticizing reality in comparison to ideals is to be found in Stirner.

The reflection of a state of reality in a system of philosophy occurs, according to Hegel, when that stage has come to an end and is about to be dialectically *aufgehoben*:

> It is only when actuality is mature that the ideal first appears over against the real and that the ideal apprehends the same real world in its substance and builds it up for itself into the shape of an intellectual realm. When philosophy paints its grey in grey, then has a shape of life grown old. By philosophy's grey in grey it cannot be rejuvenated but only understood. The owl of Minerva spreads its wings only with the falling of the dusk.[104]

Thus the very existence of the *Republic* shows that the *polis* as Plato knew it, whose rational structure he revealed in that work, was about to come to an end. By the same token, the civilization described by Hegel in his work is, he is aware, about to be transcended. Thus Hegel did not think, as his is sometimes accused of thinking,[105] that the process of history was complete in his own time.

For Hegel, philosophy is retrospective rather than

---

101 Knox, *Hegel's Philosophy of Right*, p. 11.
102 *Ibid.*
103 *Ibid.*, p. 10.
104 *Ibid.*, p. 13.
105 Foster, *The Political Philosophies of Plato and Hegel*, p. 202 n.

prospective: it looks backward to try and grasp the process whereby reality arrived at its present state; it does not forecast the future. Hegel did not see the course of history as a quasi-mechanical development, bound to run in a particular pattern; had he done so, he could easily have extended it into the future. The pattern he discerned in history does not lend itself to this sort of extension: this is the increasing realization of freedom from the time of the Oriental empires, when it was recognized that one (the despot) is free; through the classical period, when it was recognized that some (the citizens) are free; to the modern period, when it is grasped that all men as men are free.[106] The development obviously cannot proceed any farther along this line, and this has led to the conclusion that Hegel thought history had come to an end. But he explicitly says that "America is...the land of the future, where, in the ages that lie before us, the burden of the World's History shall reveal itself—perhaps in a contest between North and South America."[2107] The "perhaps" indicated that while Hegel expects the progress of history to continue, he does not feel competent to predict, with any certainty, what that future progress will bring. The dialectic of the increasing realization of freedom was the most adequate perspective upon the past that was available to Hegel; the philosopher of the future, who looks back over the development up to *his* time will have to choose some other principle, but one which is broad enough to include this progression of freedom. What that new principle might be, Hegel cannot say, because it is not yet in existence.

Nature, for Hegel, is an external manifestation or objectification of Spirit. The exact sense in which this is so is not clear; Meuller admits that the transition from Spirit to nature is "unintelligible" to him.[108] Hegel says that "the Idea freely releases itself in absolute self-security and self-repose"[109] into nature; this

---

106 Hegel, *The Philosophy of History*, p. 18.
107 *Ibid.*, p. 86.
108 Mueller, *Hegel: The Encyclopedia of Philosophy*, p. 162.
109 Johnston and Struthers, *Hegel's Science of Logic*, II, 486.

resembles Plotinian emanation. But remembering the dialectic, we can venture a guess as to Hegel's meaning. Each entity is what it is only because it is distinct from its opposite, thus it can exist only if its opposite exists. There is no temporal sequence here: remove his slave, and the master at once ceases to exist as a master. Similarly, the fundamental reality is Spirit; but Spirit is what it is only in relation to its contrary, nature. Spirit does not somehow "give rise" to nature; the two are coeternal. We further recall that all such views are essentially one-sided, and that what was at first opposed is really one and the same. Nature and Spirit, then, are not ultimately opposed, but are two sides of the same reality.

This idea of the objectification of Spirit in matter lays the foundation for Marx's view of the intimate dialectic between man and nature which constitutes *praxis*, and can be detected in his theory of value as objectified labor.

Hegel's philosophy of nature is not in good repute today. The reasons are that Hegel "disregarded" his own logic by "interfering" with his dialectic in the "formal-logical method and object problems of the sciences," and that he "encumbered his philosophy with sciences of his day and age," with the result that "he was soon outmoded and full of dead wood."[110]

Hegel, however, was determined to apply his dialectical method to the whole field of human experience, the locus of reality's consciousness of itself. According to Hegel, the natural scientist operates at a level lower than that of reason (*Vernunft*) , namely, the level of understanding (*Verstand*). The method of the understanding is traditional formal logic, which utilized fixed categories and applies them to fixed, distinct objects.[111] Reason proceeds according to the dialectical method, which dissolves these fixed determinations.[112] The results obtained by the sciences are the best of which the human mind is capable at that stage in history. But these results have not been philosophically

---

110 Mueller, *Hegel: Encyclopedia of Philosophy*, p. 165.
111 *Ibid.*, sec. 1, p. 67; sec. 5, p. 70; secs. 14-15 p. 82.
112 Johnston and Struthers, Hegel's Science of Logic, I, 36.

comprehended until they have been integrated into the philosophical systems by the dialectical method, which "retains and includes the formal logic of [understanding']."[113] The goal is not to make new scientific discoveries, but to appropriate and integrate the discoveries that have been made and are accepted by the most advanced scientific minds of the time. Hegel absolutizes these findings, but this does not mean that he regarded the science of his time as the final truth; it was just the best that was available to him.

Oddly, Mueller insists that *Verstand* is to be translated "reason," and *Vernunft* as "understanding" (p. 4 n.). This flies in the face of standard usage. Therefore, I have interchanged the English words and indicated the substitution by means of square brackets.

By another dialectical transition, Spirit returns to itself as the human mind, or Subjective Spirit. In the *Phenomenology*, Hegel examines some of the transformations undergone by human consciousness; we can deal here with only two of these. In "Lordship and Bondage" (*Herrschaft und Knechtschaft*), two self-consciousnesses encounter each other and demand recognition; a "war to the death" ensues, but stops short of this outcome when one self-consciousness submits totally, debasing itself in its recognition of the other. A dialectical reversal occurs, however, when the bondsman, through his creation of material products for the lord, finds that his own personality has been objectified and thereby established as real: while the lord, conversely, finds himself totally dependent upon this production by his servant.[114] This relation between master and servant is the prototype for the relations, in Marx, between the bourgeoisie and the proletariat; the idea of labor as the objectification and self-creation of the personality is also to be found in Marx.

The "Unhappy Consciousness" (*unglückliches Bewusstsein*), or medieval mentality is divided against itself. It perceives within

---

113 Mueller, *Hegel: Encyclopedia of Philosophy*, sec. 16 p. 84.
114 Hegel, *The Phenomenology of Mind*, pp. 228-240.

itself two opposed aspects, a changeable and an unchangeable one; it identifies itself with the former, and projects the latter into a transcendent realm, personifying it as God. It demeans itself in comparison to this "being," never realizing that this is a relationship to a part of itself.[115] This is the root of the theory of alienation to the Young Hegelians, including Stirner and Marx.

Once again there is a transition: Spirit again realizes itself in the external world, this time in the form of "Objective Spirit," or human activities and institutions. Hegel's treatment of this sphere has two aspects: a "vertical" or static dialectical analysis of the ideas of morality, law, and the state; and a dynamic account of the development and interplay of states and peoples through time. The former is the subject matter of the *Philosophy of Right*, and the latter of the Philosophy of *History*.

This Philosophy of Right deals with the will, the basis of Objective Spirit: will is "a special way of thinking, thinking translating itself into existence, thinking as the urge to give itself existence."[116] Hegel discerns three levels of moments of will: "Abstract Right" (*das Abstrakte Recht*), "Morality" (*Moralität*), and "Ethical Life" (*Sittlichkeit*).

Abstract Right comprises the basic legal-economic categories of property, contract, and wrong. In regard to Marx's contention that he turned Hegel "on his feet" by substituting materialism for idealism, it is pertinent to note, with Marcuse, that "at its roots, the *Philosophy of Right* is materialist in approach. Hegel exposes in paragraph after paragraph the social and economic under-structure of his philosophical concepts."[117] In taking possession of property, the individual puts his will into an external thing, which thereby becomes and embodiment of his personality.[2][118]Here is another source of Marx's view that man makes himself by his productive labor; the concept of property is also

---

115 *Ibid.*, pp. 251-267.
116 Knox, *Hegel's Philosophy of Right*, p. 226 (addition to sec. 2).
117 Marcuse, *Reason and Revolution*, p. 184.
118 Knox, *Hegel's Philosophy of Right*, secs. 54-58, pp. 46-48.

fundamental for Stirner. After taking possession, the individual goes on to use or consume his property, thereby asserting its inherent worthlessness in relation to his own personality; no material thing is adequate to embody fully the human spirit.[119] In Marx, this process becomes perverted and the object asserts its independence of, and dominates, the person; this is alienation as the "fetishism of commodities." In Stirner, the connection between property and personality is so close that he can speak of the individual "using himself up." The next stage is alienation (*Entäusserung*) of property, in which the individual removes his will from it and yields it to someone else.[120] This is the basis of the fetishism of commodities for Marx: the individual no longer uses his product himself, but alienates it to another; this other, the capitalist, then alienates the thing again, to the merchant, and so on. The result is that inanimate objects take on a life of their own; they are no longer under human control, but behave according to the quasi-natural laws of economics. Hegel remarks that the abilities of the person himself can be alienated to another; this alienation, however, must be limited in time, or else the person has sold himself into slavery.[121] Here can be seen a precursor of Marx's doctrine that the worth of a commodity is the labor time required to produce it, as well as his protest against the lengthening of the working day.[122]

In discussing alienation of labor, Hegel makes the following comment: "force is the totality of its manifestations, substance of its accidents, the universal of its particulars."[123] This is an example of Hegel's notion of the concrete universal (*konkretes Allgemeines*), which has a fundamental ambiguity, and which was interpreted differently by Stirner and Marx. There is no Platonic universal in separation from its particulars: "For a person is a

119 *Ibid.*, sec. 59, p. 49.
120 *Ibid.*, secs. 65-66, pp. 52-53.
121 *Ibid*, sec. 67, p. 54
122 Marcuse, *Reason and Revolution*, p. 195.
123 Knox, *Hegel's Philosophy of Right*, remark to sec. 67, p. 54.

specific existence; not man in general (a term to which no real existence corresponds) but a particular human being";[124] without which its particulars the universal would not exist. But neither is the universal just the collection of the particulars: each particular bears the universal within itself, and this constitutes its most important aspect. Hegel says in the *Logic*:

> In an object the nature, peculiar essence, the truly permanent and substantial among the multiplicity and contingency of its appearance and fleeting manifestation, consists in the...Universal immanent in it; as every human individual, though infinitely unique, is so only *because* it belongs to the class of man, every animal only *because* it belongs to the class of animal....[125]

This concept could be taken as meaning that no particular is independent, but is related to all others of its kind in its very essence; Marx took it this way, and described the nature of man as inherently social. Or it could be taken in the opposite sense, as meaning that each particular, as bearing the universal within it, is totally independent of all others. Stirner inclined toward this interpretation; and since the universal no longer served to relate particular, or any other purpose, he eliminated it from his ontology.

Hegel goes on to discuss contract, in which two wills meet to exchange equal values of property;[126] non-malicious or civil wrong, in which there is honest disagreement between the parties as to the facts of the exchange;[127] fraud, in which one party consciously attempts to bring about an unequal exchange, while pretending to bring his will into harmony with that of

---

124 Hegel, *The Philosophy of History*, p. 24.
125 Johnston and Struthers, *Hegel's Science of Logic*, I, 45.
126 Knox, *Hegel's Philosophy of Right*, secs. 72-81, pp. 57-64.
127 *Ibid.*, secs. 84-86. p. 65.

the other;[128] and crime, in which there is not even a "show" of agreement, but one party uses coercion to deprive the other of his property.[129] Hegel endorses the retributive theory of punishment: the criminal, as a rational being, implicitly demands to have his act of coercion annulled by another such act exerted against him; the deterrent and rehabilitative theory regard the criminal as an animal.[130]

But the criminal and the punishing agency are still two separate entities; by a dialectical negation, punishment is made internal, and the transition from Right to Morality is affected.[131] This is essentially the level of Kantian moral theory, in which ethical conduct is determined by the self-legislating reason of the individual, in opposition to his inclinations. Hegel points out that Kant's categorical imperative is so empty of content that is can make any act at all a duty;[132] the state cannot make such subjective conviction the basis of law, which must be universal.[133]

Hegel turns to the third level of Objective Spirit, Ethical Life, in which the individual's subjective will is in harmony with objective institutions which give it content.[134] The first phase here is the family, in which individuals lose their particularity and become part of a whole through marriage and child-rearing;[135] the family property, owned in common, is the external embodiment of this unity, as individual property was the embodiment of the individual personality.[136]

The family dissolves when the children reach maturity,[137] and the marks the transition to the sphere of civil society (*bürgerliche*

---

128 *Ibid.*, secs. 87-89, pp. 65-66.
129 *Ibid.*, secs. 90-99, pp. 66-70.
130 *Ibid.*, secs. 100-102, pp. 71-72.
131 *Ibid.*, secs. 103-104, pp. 73-74.
132 *Ibid.*, sec. 135, pp. 89-90.
133 *Ibid.*, remark to sec. 13, p. 91.
134 *Ibid.*, sec. 142, p. 105.
135 *Ibid.*, secs. 158-169, pp. 110-116.
136 *Ibid.*, secs. 170-172, pp. 116-117.
137 *Ibid.*, sec. 178, p. 119.

Gesellschaft). This is the realm of particularity, in which each individual strives to attain his own ends without corner for others; but, by a dialectical reversal, this very egoism unites them into a "system of complete interdependence" in which the well-being of each depends upon the activities of others.[138] This is Hegel's account of the economic sector of the society of his time; Marx adapted it from its semi-feudal context as a description of capitalism, and regarded the opposition between individual self-interest and universal interdependence as one of the contradictions which doomed the capitalist order to destruction. Stirner saw the atomistic egoism of this level as the truth of human existence.

The individual's relation to the whole of civil society is mediated by the existence of certain groups of which he is a part:

> The infinitely complex, crisscross, movement of reciprocal production and exchange and the equally infinite multiplicity of means therein employed, become crystallized...and distinguished into general groups. As a result, the entire complex is build up into particular systems of needs, means, and types of work relative to these needs, modes of satisfaction and of theoretical and practical education, i.e. into systems, to one or the other of which individuals are assigned—in other words, into class divisions [*Stände*].[139]

Hegel has here prefigured Marx's notion of the formation of classes through division of labor, but the classes recognized by Hegel are different from those in Marx: the agricultural class,[140] the business class (which includes all those engaged in manufacture and trade),[141] and the "universal class" (*der allgemeine Stand*) of civil servants, which "has for its task the universal interests of

---

138 *Ibid.*, secs. 182-183, pp. 122-123.
139 *Ibid.*, sec. 201, pp. 130-131.
140 *Ibid.*, sec. 203, p. 131.
141 *Ibid.*, sec. 204, p. 132.

the community."[142] Marx retains the notion of a universal class; for him, this is the proletariat.

One of the functions of the class of civil servants is to deal with the poor; here Hegel makes some comments which reappear, greatly elaborated and expressed in more technical terminology, in Marx:

> When the standard of living of a large mass of people falls below a certain subsistence level... the result is the creation of a rabble of paupers. At the same time this brings with it, at the other end of the social scale, conditions which greatly facilitate the concentration of disproportionate wealth in a few hands.[143]

This is a precursor of Marx's theories of the polarization of classes and the increasing misery of the proletariat. Hegel continues that the situation could be remedied through charity or public support, or through job creation, but

> in this even the volume of production would be increased, but the evil consists perceivably in an excess of production and in the lack of a proportionate number of consumers who are themselves also producers, and thus it is simply intensified by both of the methods...by which it is sought to alleviate it.[144]

This is an anticipation of Marx's theory of underconsumption as productive of crises under capitalism. "It hence become apparent that despite an excess of wealth civil society is not rich enough, i.e. its own resources are insufficient to check excessive poverty and the creation of a pernicious rabble."[145] "this inner

---

142 *Ibid.*, sec. 205, p. 132.
143 *Ibid.*, sec. 244, p. 150.
144 *Ibid.*, sec. 245, p. 150.
145 *Ibid.*

dialectic of civil society thus drive it—or at any rate it drives a specific civil society—to push beyond its own limits and seek marks, and so its necessary means of subsistence, in other lands... ."[146] Thus underconsumption leads to foreign trade, foreign investment, and colonization, as in Marx. Marx goes beyond Hegel here, however, and sees that these foreign adventures are only a temporary remedy which ultimately aggravates the situation and leads to the downfall of capitalism.

The most rational phase of Objective Spirit is the state. It is the universal moment which negates and transcends the particularity of civil society. Controversy has arisen as to whether Hegel is idealizing his contemporary Prussia as the final and most perfect form of state. The solution to this dispute has already been indicated in the account of Hegel's conception of philosophy: he was seeking to understand his time and place, but he wanted to relate that time and place to the whole of reality, as a partial manifestation of Spirit. He wanted to find in the government of the state where he lived the rational core, however surrounded it might be by accidents and imperfections this is the Idea of the state. While the Prussian form of government was the fullest expression of reason that Hegel knew, it was not as full an expression as it might have been. Hegel's conservative followers recognized the former point; his radical followers seized upon the latter, and sought to make the state conform more fully to the rational ideal implicit in it. Hegel's position would have been that the positions of both camps were untenable: the very existence of his own political philosophy revealed that it was "the falling of the dusk," that the Prussian state was about to be transcended in ways no one could predict. Furthermore, Hegel's state was conceived as the dialectical negation of a specific economic order, that of civil society;[147] they would both change together. Thus there is a basis in Hegel's thought for Marx's view of an impending socio-economic revolution.

---

146 *Ibid.*, sec. 246, p. 151.
147 Marcuse, *Reason and Revolution*, p. 202.

Hegel's state is authoritarian, as the antithesis of anarchistic civil society. But the authority is not perceived as a purely external one: the individual accepts the laws as expressions of his own will, and so in harmony with it.[148] To Stirner, this idea of the state is an example of alienation: the individual permits himself to be dominated by something that is essentially his own creation. Hegel frequently refers to the state as an "organism" (*Organismus*),[149] as a whole which is an intimate unity, rather than a mere collection, of its parts; the citizens and branches of government are analogous to the organs of a living thing, in which all are subordinated to the welfare of the whole. This universalistic, organistic view of the state is repeated in Marx, who, however, does not regard it as exemplified by the existing state; the goal of revolution is to create such an organism on the level of civil society, in which event the state, as a separate structure, will be superfluous.

On the other hand Hegel retains his principle that the only real being are individuals:

"A so-called 'artificial person', be it a society, a community, or a family, however inherently concrete it may be, contains personality only abstractly, as one moment of itself."[150] Thus a true individual the monarch, "the absolute apex of an organically developed state,"[151] is needed to place his will in each act of the legislature in order for it to become law.

When the laws have been made by the legislature and enacted by the monarch, they are enforced by the executive, which is the class of civil servants.[152] The legislature itself consists of the monarch and the executive, plus the Estates (*das ständliche Element*), the representatives of the agricultural and business classes.[153] The Estates act as a safeguard against possible tyranny on the part of

---

148 Knox, *Hegel's Philosophy of Right*, sec. 261. P. 161.
149 *Ibid.*, sec. 259 p. 180; sec. 267, p. 163; sec. 269, p. 164 etc.
150 *Ibid.*, remark to sec. 279, p. 182.
151 *Ibid.*, remark to sec. 286, p. 188.
152 *Ibid.*, sec. 300, p. 195; sec. 305-307, pp. 199-200.
153 *Ibid.*, sec. 300, p. 195; secs. 305-306, p. 199; sec. 309, p. 200.

the monarch or of the executive, but do not really "represent" the interests of their constituents, as these particularistic and so out of keeping with the universal nature of the state.[154] The function of the institutions of public opinion, free speech and the press, is not to allow the interests of the masses to influence the deliberations of government, but the reverse. These institutions act as "safety valves," as it were, for public passions, enabling the citizens to be more easily reconciled to government policies.[155] This dialectical reversal of the supposed functions of free speech and press is accepted by Stirner, who rejects these institutions for this reason.

The analysis of the concept of the state ends with an account of international relations, which reproduce on a larger scale the anarchy of civil society.[156] An obvious dialectical transition would have called for the unification of these states into a super-state or a world government, as a civil society called for its transcendence into the state. Hegel's failure to make this transition has been credited to his nationalistic sentiments.[157] But the real reason, obviously, is simply that there was no such government in Hegel's time; it did not exist, and so was not available to be incorporated into a philosophical account of reality.

Hegel's static analysis of the dialectical relationships between the elements of the state is succeeded by a dynamic account of the rise and fall of states through history, leading up to the present.[158] This development is depicted at greater length, and in somewhat different terms, in the Philosophy of History. Each nation is the embodiment of a specific level of development of Spirit; as Spirit progresses, different nations succeed one another as the dominant ones of the world stage, depending on which is

---

154 *Ibid.*, secs. 316-318, pp. 204-205.
155 *Ibid.*, sec. 319, pp. 205-206.
156 *Ibid.*, secs. 322-329, pp. 208-212.
157 Sidney Hook, "Hegel Rehabilitated?" in Kaufmann, *Hegel's Political Philosophy*, p. 64.
158 Knox, *Hegel's Philosophy of Right*, sec. 341-360, pp. 216-223.

the vehicle of Spirit at that time. This dominance is primarily cultural, though it may include political dominance (as it did with the Romans, but not with the Greeks).[159]

The analysis thus far has been on a general level, concerned with the spirit of an entire nation or people. But, again, for Hegel, the only actual existent are individuals; and so the transitions from one level to another turn out to be effect by "world-historical individuals," such as Alexander, Caesar, and Napoleon. These are the men who sense what the time call for, are obsessed by this idea, and are driven by the passion to attain it. Their deeds are often bloody and cruel, and result in war and suffering; history is "the slaughter-bench at which the happiness of peoples, the wisdom of States, and the virtue of individuals have been victimized."[160] Nor do these world-historical individuals themselves derive happiness from their vocation: "their whole life was labor and trouble," and "when their object is attained they fall off like empty hulls from the kernel."[161] But through all of this the "cunning of reason" (*List der Vernunft*), which uses these men and peoples as its instruments, attains its goal.[162] It is futile to resist it: Brutus assassinated Caesar in order to restore the Republic, and the result was the Empire.[163] Nor are the actions of these individuals to be judged by the standards of morality: these standards are relative to the level currently achieved, and that level is about to be transcended.[164]

In Marx, the notions of world-historical individuals and peoples coalesce in the intermediate level of generality of the world-historical class; and he shares Hegel's view of the relativism of morality. For Stirner, history is made only by individuals;

---

159 Shlomo Avineri "Hegel and Nationalism," in Kaufmann, *Hegel's Political Philosophy*, pp. 129-130.

160 Hegel, *The Philosophy of History*, p. 21.

161 *Ibid.*, p. 31.

162 *Ibid.*, p. 33.

163 *Ibid.*, p. 313.

164 *Ibid.*, pp. 34-35.

Philip Breed Dematteis

he, too, accepts the notion that morality is not absolute.

Finally, the sphere of Objective Spirit is transcended by that of Absolute Spirit, the cultural activities of art, religion, and philosophy. These take place only in a civilized state, and are relative to the level of development of the people. Hegel says:

> It is thus *One Individuality* which, presented in its essence as God, is honored and enjoyed in *Religion*; which is exhibited as an object of sensuous contemplation in *Art*; and is apprehended as an intellectual conception, in *Philosophy*. In virtue of the original identity of their essence, purport, and object, these various forms are inseparably united with the Spirit of the State. Only in connection with this particular religion, can this particular political constitution exist; just as in such or such a State, such or such a Philosophy or order of Art.[165]

Marx's materialist interpretation of history also holds that the cultural pursuits of religion, art, and philosophy are relative to the time in which they exist; for him, these activities are determined by the character of economic production at the given time.

6. The Split among Hegel's Students

At his death in 1831, Hegel left a large following of students who accepted his method and many of his conclusions. The vast sweep and deep ambiguity of his system, however, called for a certain type of mind to hold together the synthesis he had effected. Few of these were to be found after Hegel departed the scene, and in the first decade after his death, the internal stresses of his thought broke apart in the form of fragmentation of the Hegelian school.

The two main points of divergence were religion and politics. Hegel's position on these subjects was ambiguous in the extreme,

---

165 *Ibid.*, p. 53.

Max Stirner Versus Karl Marx

at least to minds with less subtlety and penetration than his own. In politics, his dictum that "what is rational is actual and what is actual is rational" was open to two interpretations: if the second clause is emphasized, the consequence is political conservatism; emphasis upon the first clause, together with a conviction that the prevailing political and social order is not rational, leads to a radical mission to remake the world according to a rational pattern.[166] In religion, Hegel has said that it has the same content as philosophy, with the former expressing this content in mythical and imaginative, the latter in rational, language. The question now was whether religion misrepresented a non-theistic (pantheistic or atheistic) position in theistic terms, or whether philosophy misrepresented a theistic position in non-theistic terms.

It was along these two lines that the split into right, center, and left Hegelianism occurred. The right Hegelians generally inclined toward political conservatism and theological orthodoxy; the center tried to preserve Hegel's influence and to apply his method to various fields of specialization, such as law, history of philosophy, and aesthetics; while the left, or "Young" Hegelians advanced revolutionary political views and humanist, naturalist, and atheist philosophies of religion. The situation is blurred somewhat by the fact that some of the same individuals had a foot in both of the extreme camps, siding with one party on religion matters and with the other on political questions. It is certain that Stirner and Marx belong to the Young Hegelian wing, and can be seen as two opposed end-points of its development. The next section will summarize some of the steps in the transformation of Hegelianism which led up to the positions of Stirner and Marx.

7. The Young Hegelians

In general, the Young Hegelians were middle-class intellectuals,

---

166 Löwith, *From Hegel to Nietzsche*, p. 68

most of whom studied at the University of Berlin and there came under the influence of Hegelianism. Many of them had intended to become professors, but were prohibited from doing so for various reasons, including the conservative political situation. Their existence centered around informal gatherings such as the *Doktorenklub* in Berlin, through which Marx was converted to Hegelianism, and its successor, *Die Freien*, of which Stirner was a member; and around various short lived newspapers and reviews which some of them edited, and to which all of them contributed.[167]

The general tactic pursued by the Young Hegelians was to turn Hegel's dialectical method against what they took to be his orthodox religious and conservative political conclusions. Sometimes they represented this as an interpretation of Hegel's own esoteric view, which he had concealed, sometimes as a deliberate extension of Hegel's method beyond the limits to which he had been prepared to go. They saw the dialectic, with its stress of negativity, as a revolutionary method: it entailed constant criticism of the existing order, and allowed no final synthesis.[168]

The attack upon religion was the first step in this process, and later, when the government reacted against this attack by closing their journals and denying them teaching positions, they carried the assault to the state itself.

In 1835, David Friedrich Strauss, in *The Life of Jesus*, showed that the Gospels were so riddled with inconsistencies that they could not be accepted as literal reports of facts. They were rather, as Hegel had said of religion in general, the mythical expression of the level of consciousness of a people at a certain stage of development. In the myth of the incarnation of God in Christ, the early Christian community was unconsciously expressing the unity of God and man; but their level of development allowed them to conceive of the divine as exemplified in only one individual. The

---

167 David McLellan, *The Young Hegelians and Karl Marx* (New York and Washington: Frederick A. Praeger, 1969), pp. 4-9.
168 Dupré, *The Philosophical Foundations of Marxism*, pp. 70-71

myth must now be reinterpreted, according to Strauss, to bring out the truth hidden in it: that the human race as a whole—humanity as such—is the manifestation of the divine.[169]

Bruno Bauer, who at first joined in the general denunciation of Strauss, later came to an even more radical position. He decided that each of the Gospels was the product of a single individual, a work of art, in which the truth that consciousness is superior to nature presented in an imaginative manner. But these imaginative representations, which were an advance in their time over previous conceptions, had become solidified as dogmas which fettered the further development of self-consciousness. They must, therefore, be rejected in favor of atheism: there is no God, no higher reality than human self-conciousness.[170]

For Ludwig Feuerbach, religion was an example of alienation, in the sense that Hegel had elaborated in his depiction of the "unhappy consciousness"; but Hegel was himself guilty of this misconception. Both idealism and Christianity erect a part of man's own nature as supreme and dominant over him. In idealism, this part is the consciousness, which is really only one aspect of the total human being; man is essentially part of nature, and so material. The mistake was due to an improper analysis of sense perception, which was regarded as merely a mode of though; in fact, it is man's means of communication with nature, and so his basic mode of cognition.[171] In religion, alienation came from recognizing that the attributes of human nature are present in the individual in only a limited way; to avoid the shame of acknowledging these limitations as strictly his own, the individual attributes them to all men, and projects the attributes in unlimited form upon an imaginary being. Instead, he should see that these attributes and potentialities are present in unlimited form in the human species, in humanity as a whole. Thus the love of

169 David Friedrich Strauss, *The Life of Jesus*, trans. From the 4th German ed. by George Eliot (4th ed.; London: S. Sonnenschein, 1902)
170 McLellan, *The Young Hegelians and Karl Marx*, pp. 55-58
171 Dupré, *The Philosophical Foundations of Marxism*, pp. 72-73

God really means the love of mankind, and Christianity is to be replaced by a religion of humanity.[172]

The possibility of utilizing Hegelianism for social change depended on its being not just retrospective, as Hegel himself had held, but capable of projection into the future. August von Cieszkowski showed how this could be done: the pattern of development up to the present is a portion of the whole; the rest of that whole—the future—can be predicted in its broad outlines, just as a paleontologist can reconstruct from a bone the general appearance of an animal. Each period in history has had a vision of the future peculiar to its stage of development. The mode of prediction in the present, according to Cieszkowski, is social action, or *praxis*: the future must be brought into being by the conscious, willful interaction of man with nature.[173]

Arnold Ruge, advancing this practical orientation, regarded the Hegelian system as the highest manifestation of reason; what remained was to make reason actual in social life by subjecting the existing state to criticism insofar as it fell short of the ideal of universality as described by Hegel. He attempted to effect this by founding several radical journals, expecting the publication of such philosophical criticism to stimulate the existence of a political opposition in Germany.[174]

Moses Hess, acknowledging his debt to Cieszkowski, stressed the need to make philosophy prospective rather than retrospective, to bring its vision of the future into realization through practice. The negative, theoretical criticism carried out by Ruge and the contributors to his journals was not sufficient; only a small circle of intellectuals would be reached this way. Philosophy must

---

172 Ludwig Feuerbach, *The Essence of Christianity*, trans. from the 2nd German ed. by Marian Evans (New York: C. Blanchard, 1955).

173 McLellan, *The Young Hegelians and Karl Marx*, pp. 9-11; Avineri, *The Social and Political Thought of Karl Marx*, pp. 124-130.

174 Avineri, *The Social and Political Thought of Karl Marx*, p. 132; Stephen D. Crites, "Hegelianism," *The Encyclopedia of Philosophy*, ed. Paul Edwards (8 Vols.; New York: The Macmillan Company and The Free Press, 1967), III, 452-453.

be translated into social action; the goal is a revolution leading to communism.[175]

Both of these strains of the Young Hegelian transformation of Hegelianism, the critique of religion as an alienation of the human essence, and the dialectical criticism of the existing social and political conditions, are taken over, applied in different ways, and extended by Stirner and Marx.

175 Avineri, *The Social and Political Thought of Karl Marx*, p. 153; McLellan, *The Young Hegelians and Karl Marx*, pp. 141-145; Hook, *From Hegel to Marx*, pp. 188-205.

Max Stirner Versus Karl Marx

Chapter II

THE RADICAL INDIVIDUALISM OF MAX STIRNER

Max Stirner carried the radical criticism of the Young Hegelians to its furthest extreme; he eliminated all universals, including the state, society, and humanity; all moral values; and all supreme beings. All of these he considered examples of "alienation," mental products which men had allowed to dominate them. For Stirner, the only reality was the individual, with a multitude of qualities; "consciousness," so dear to Hegel and the Young Hegelians, was merely one of these attributes.

1. Life[176] and Early Writings

He was born in Bayreuth in 1806, as Johann Kaspar Schmidt. He attended the local Gymnasium, where he was usually among the first six of his class, and passed the Leaving Examination third out of twenty-five, with the commendation "very worthy." It was during his school days that he acquired the nickname "Stirner,"

---

176 John Henry Mackay, *Max Stirner: Sein Leben und sein Werk* (Berlin: Verlag von Schuster & Loeffler, 1898).

due to his unusually high forehead (*Stirn*).[177]

He entered the Philosophy Department at the University of Berlin in 1826, where for the next two years he studied logic, Greek literature, geography, ethics, theology, dogmatics, and ecclesiastical history, and attended Hegel's lectures on the history of philosophy, philosophy of religion, and philosophy of spirit.

Stirner went to the University of Erlangen in 1828, and to the University of Königsberg the following year, but attended no lectures at the latter institution. His mother was beginning to lose her mind, and Stirner neglected his studies for the next two years in order to care for her. He then returned to Berlin in 1832 to finish his education and qualify for a teaching position; however, he fell ill and had to neglect sever of his courses in order to prepare for his final examinations.

Stirner took his written examination in November. He was poorly prepared for these examinations, largely due to the time he had spent caring for his mother. At this time he also presented two written tasks which had been assigned in March: a translation, with commentary, of a long section of Thucydides, and a dissertation, "On School Rules," his earliest philosophical writing to be preserved.

After his orals the following April, his examiners said that he lacked precise information on all subjects except the Bible; Trendelenburg said that his speculative ability was not match by his knowledge of the history of philosophy, especially recent philosophy. He was awarded only a conditional *facultas docendi*

---

177 The only two extant likenesses of Stirner are by Friedrich Engels. One is a caricature of a meeting of die Freien, in which Stirner is seen standing to one side, calmly smoking a cigar, while a fierce argument rages in the foreground between Arnold Ruge, on the one side, Ludwig Buhl and Bruno and Edgar Bauer, on the other. The other is a sketch done for John Henry McKay in 1892. Both are reproduced in Hans G. Helms, *Die Ideologie der anonymen Gesellschaft: Max Stirners >Einziger< und der Fortschritt des demokratischen Selbstbewusstseins vom Vormarz biz zur Bundesrepublik* (Köln: Verlag M. Du Mont Schauberg, 1966), pp. 37 and 25, respectively.

Max Stirner Versus Karl Marx

and his application for appointment was rejected by the Royal Brandenburg Commission for Schools. He spent the next eighteen months, a prolonged probationary year, teaching Latin in a private school in Berlin, without pay.

From 1837-1839, he probably tried to make up the deficiencies in his knowledge with self-instruction. In December of 1837, he married his landlady's daughter, a poorly-educated and colorless young woman who died in childbirth, along with the baby, the following August.

In 1839 he acquired his only regular teaching position at a private girls' high school in Berlin. Toward the end of that year he began to attend meeting of *die Freien*, a group of Young Hegelians, at Hippel's Weinstube in the evenings. He took little part in the discussions, but worked out his positions in silence. At these meetings, Stirner encountered Marie Dähnhardt, a liberated young woman of the time who smoked cigars, drank beer, and accompanied the men on their excursions to the brothels. She was also heiress to about 30,000 thalers. She and Stirner were married on October 21, 1843, in a rather bohemian ceremony; Stirner having forgotten to procure wedding rings, the copper rings from Bruno Bauer's purse were used.

Stirner had published articles in 1842 and 1843, and although these revealed an increasing radicalism, they were generally in line with the opinions of the other Young Hegelians. But his major work, *The Ego and His Own*, which appeared in November, 1844,[178] attacked the positions of the leading Young Hegelians, particularly Feuerbach and Bauer, and most of his friends deserted him. This was, however, his finest hour: the book created a furor in philosophical circles all over Germany; Stirner was attacked in print, and replied in kind.

---

178 Der Einzige und sein Eigenthum (Leipzig: Otto Wigand, 1845). The first 1,000-copy edition was printed and distributed quickly to avoid confiscation by the censor. Some copies were seized, but the confiscation order was soon rescinded by the Saxon Minister of Interior on the ground that the book was "too absurd" to be dangerous.

After this his fortune dwindled. He started a milk-distribution company in the summer of 1845, using his wife's inheritance as capital; this venture promptly failed, and by the following summer he was advertising for a loan. His wife left him at the end of 1846; more than forty years later, she could not speak of Stirner without bitterness. In 1847, he completed a translation of the economic writings of Adam Smith and J.B. Say, without the translator's notes he had promised. In 1852, he published History of the Reaction, an uninspired work consisting mostly of quotations from other authors. For the next few years he made a living acting as an intermediary in transactions between small businessmen, and also received payments from the sale of his mother's home. He spent some time in prison for debt.

In May, 1856, he was stung on the neck by a winged insect, and after lying in a violent fever for several weeks, he died on June 25. Bruno Bauer and Ludwig Buhl who had been witnesses at his ill-fated wedding and who had never abandoned him, were among the few mourners at his burial.

This is not, obviously, a life to be envied or emulated. It is not, however, inconsistent with Stirner's philosophy, as elaborated in *The Ego and His Own*. It is frequently taken to be so; for example, George Woodcock writes,

> Just as Schmidt assumed a new name to publish his book, so he appeared to create a new personality to write it, or at least to call up some violent, unfamiliar self that was submerged in his daily existence. For in the unhappy, luckless, and ill-ordered career of the timid Schmidt there was nothing at all of the free-standing egoist of Max Stirner's passionate dream; the contrast between the man and his work seems to provide us with a classic example of the power of literature as a compensatory daydream.[179]

179 George Woodcock, *Anarchism: A History of Libertarian Ideas and Movements* (Cleveland and New York: The World Publishing Company,

Max Stirner Versus Karl Marx

John Carroll agrees that there is a contrast between Stirner's life and his philosophical position, but recognizes that "there is too much trenchant psychology in The Ego and His Own to identify its author as a day-dreamer escaping from a society with whose practicalities he could not cope."[180] How explain the difference, then?

The answer is given by R. W. K. Paterson, who phrases it this way:

> Judgments of failure require the adoption of criteria for success. Stirner explicitly rejected not only the criteria of personal success adopted by his society and age; he rejected not only each and every criterion proposed by the most latitudinarian of his philosophical contemporaries: he rejected the very concept of a uniform criterion which could be applied to himself as The Unique One, the metaphysical hero of his central work.[181]

To judge Stirner as having fallen short in his personal existence of the ideal he described in his book, is to misinterpret that ideal. This misinterpretation probably comes from reading him in the light of Nietzsche, whose ideal was the creative individual who would accomplish great deeds if unfettered by the restrictions of society, religion, and morality. But a value-concept such as "greatness" has no place in Stirner's outlook. His concern was that the individual be inner-directed, that he choose his own life from among the possibilities open him; and this is what Stirner did. The fact that he failed at many of his chosen projects was unfortunate for him, but not inconsistent with his position. His goal was not a "successful" life, but a life free from illusions.

Another interesting facet of Stirner's biography is his sacrifice of his own prospects of a teaching career to care for his mother during her decline into madness. He rails constantly against

---

1962) p. 96.
180 Carroll, *Max Stirner: The Ego and His Own*, p. 17
181 Paterson, *The Nihilistic Egoist: Max Stirner*, pp. 16-1

self-sacrifice, and particularly against filial piety. Yet, here, too, a fuller comprehension of his position removes the appearance of contradiction. It was only self-sacrifice and filial piety as *duties* that drew his ire. Stirner objects to loving and sacrificing for abstractions, such as "humanity," "family," etc., rather than for the real individuals who are important to the egoist and whose happiness is bound up with his own.

Stirner's early writings show a definite progression toward the radical egoism of his mature work. His examination essay, "On School Rules," shows him to be strongly influenced by the dialectical method and concepts of Hegel.[182] He began publishing articles in 1842 in the various journals and magazines which served as a forum for Young Hegelian ideas, and at first his position was indistinguishable from those of his colleagues.

His first published article is a review of Bruno Bauer's anonymous book The Trumpet of the Last Judgement Against Hegel, the Atheist and Antichrist. Here Bauer had ironically "exposed" Hegel as the true enemy of religion who, by reconciling religion and philosophy and thereby eliminating mystery from the universe, had destroyed man's fear of the sacred. Stirner endorses this interpretation, and refers to the "self-sufficiency of the free man" who destroys the whole world in his murder of God, and whose self-creation is indistinguishable from his work of destruction.[183] His second article, "Reply of a Member of the Berlin Community," was a response to a tract by the fifty-seven ministers which worried about the decline in church attendance. Here Stirner, like Feuerbach, takes a position warning the churchmen that the decline in public piety will continue unless they cease preaching the servile, cowardly Christian faith, and begin teaching a humanitarian religion in which men are taught to reverence their own humanity and live by a rational ethic.[184]

---

182 Carroll, *Max Stirner: The Ego and His Own*, p. 18; Paterson, *The Nihilistic Egoist: Max Stirner*, p. 35.

183 Paterson, *The Nihilistic Egoist: Max Stirner*, pp. 49-50.

184 *Ibid.*, p. 49

Between March and October of 1842, he published a series of articles in the Rheinisch Zeitung, two of which appeared while Marx was editing the journal.[4] Most were reviews or comments on the political situation, written from the typical Young-Hegelian standpoint of social and intellectual reform, opposing the religious and political conservatism of the Prussian government.[185] He wrote a similar series for the *Leipziger allgemeine Zeitung* at about the same time.

It was in the Rheinische Zeitung that two of his four major earlier writings appears: "The False Principle of Our Education," and "Art and Religion."[186] The first writing deals with the disputes then going on in educational circles as to the relative merits of classical and practical education. Stirner finds both inadequate, as they are merely concerned with imparting knowledge, not with creating self-reliant individuals. Here can be seen the Young Hegelian idea, originated by Cieszkowski, that the next transformation of history will see theory turned into practice, knowledge into will:

> If it is the drive of our time, after *freedom of thought* is won, to pursue it to that perfection through which it changes to *freedom of the will* in order to realize the latter as the principle of a new era, then the final goal of education can no longer be *knowledge*, but the will born out of knowledge, and the spoken expression of that for which it has to strive is: the *personal* or *free man*.[187]

---

185 Carroll, *Max Stirner: The Ego and His Own*, p. 21.

186 *Ibid.*, p. 50.

187 Max Stirner, *The False Principle of Our Education, or Humanism and Realism*, trans. Robert H. Beebe; ed. with annotation and an introduction by James J. Martin (Colorado Springs, Colorado: Ralph Miles, 1967), p. 21; John Henry Mackay (ed.), *Max Stirners kleinere Schriften und seine Entgegnungen auf die Kritik seines Werkes: "Der Einzige und sein Eigenthum." Aus den Jahren 1842-1847*. Herausgegeben von John Henry Mackay. (Berlin: Schuster & Loeffler, 1898), p. 21.

Philip Breed Dematteis

Stirner advocates making use of "childlike obstinacy and in-
tractability," which "have as much right as childlike curiosity. The
latter is being stimulated; so one shall also call forth the natural
strength of the will, *opposition*." But teachers are loath to do this;
the pupils may rise up against them. Stirner's answer to this objection is a portent of his later call for universal egoism, in which
no one will be dominant or subservient:

> If pride turns into spite, then the child approaches me
> with violence; I do not have to endure this since I am
> just as free as the child. Must I however, defend myself
> against him by using the convenient rampart of author-
> ity? No, I oppose him with the strength of my own free-
> dom; this the spite of the child will break up by itself.
> Whoever is a complete person does not need—to be an
> authority.[188]

In "Art and Religion," Stirner takes up the Feuerbachian
theme of alienation; the essay appeared only a few months after the publication of *The Essence of Christianity*.[189] Here the
Hegelian notion of the unity of art and religion is given a new
twist: both of them are examples of alienation. The artist exter-
nalizes human ideals and aspirations onto the work of art, which
then, as a material object, stands over against its creator and his
whole species; religion takes over this content, but removes its
sensuous manifestation, "spiritualizes" it, and thereby makes it
all the more enslaving.[190] The solution to alienation, which has
been responsible for "all the torments, all the struggles of centuries,"[191] is, for Stirner as for Feuerbach, for man to bring his

---

188 Stirner, *The False Principle of Our Education*, p. 26; Mackay, *Max Stirners
kleinere Schriften*, p. 27.

189 Paterson, *The Nihilistic Egoist: Max Stirner*, p. 53.

190 Mackay, *Max Stirners kleinere Schriften*, p. 25; Carroll, *Max Stirner: The
Ego and His Own*, pp. 231-232.

191 Mackay, *Max Stirners kleinere Schriften*, p. 37; Carroll, *Max Stirner: The*

ideals back within himself, where they had their origin. Here "man" is still humanity as a whole. In Stirner's later work, where alienation plays the central role, it becomes the individual man; and Feuerbach's "humanity" becomes one more alienation to be overcome.

The third and fourth of Stirner's major formative articles were written by the summer of 1843 for the projected journal *Berliner Monatsschrift*; publication was delayed by the censorship until 1845, at which time the one and only issue, containing both of Stirner's pieces, came out.

The first of these, "Some Preliminaries on the Love-State," was a commentary on a memorandum by the statesman von Stein, which attributed Germany's losses in the Napoleonic Wars to the political backwardness of the Germans, and advocated constitutional changes allowing popular representation. These proposals had never been put into effect, much to the consternation of German liberals. Stirner, however, saw that the "equality" recommended by von Stein was really just an equality of subjects, and that his "liberty" was the liberty of the subjects to perform their duties to the state. The freer the state—that is, the less it relied on coercion and more on social good will (which Stirner regarded as a secular version of Christian love), the more enslaved was the citizen.[192] This critique of the paradoxes of liberalism is carried on at greater length in *The Ego and His Own*.

The final article is a review by Stirner of a melodramatic novel of the time Eugène Sue's *Les Mystères de Paris*. The novel had attracted the attention of social critics, including Marx,[193] because of its depiction of the miserable living conditions of the poor in Paris. In his review, Stirner develops his critique of moral values: all of the characters are enslaved by principles of one kind

---

Ego and His Own, p. 232.

192 Mackay, *Max Stirners kleinere Schriften*, pp. 71-80; Paterson, *The Nihilistic Egoist: Max Stirner*, pp. 54-56.

193 In *The Holy Family*, chapter 8; Karl Marx and Friedrich Engels, *Werke* (38+II Vols.; Berlin: Dietz Verlag, 1961-1971), pp. 172-213.

or another, whether or virtue or of vice; and this brings them to their bad ends. To this Stirner opposes his "self-made man" who stands above all such superstitious notions of good and evil, virtue and sin, and freely chooses his own style of life.[194]

Stirner reaches the culmination of his radicalism, and pulls together the threads of his religious, moral, and political criticisms, in his major work, *The Ego and His Own*.

2. The Ego and His Own:[195] Structure and Method

At first reading *The Ego and His Own* appears to have very little coherent structure at all: "It often presents the appearance of notes taken at random and put down with no attempt at co-ordination."[196] Stirner admits that two sections of the book were written in precisely this way. The same practice is self-evident in several other places.

Closer examination, however, places the structure of the work definitely within the Hegelian tradition. After a brief prologue, the book is divided into two major parts, titled "Man" and "I"; these correspond to the divisions of Feuerbach's *Essence of Christianity* into "God" and "Man."[197] Feuerbach had presented God as an alienated projection of the human essence, to be abolished in favor of the human essence itself. Stirner sets out to apply the same treatment to Feuerbach's Man, replacing it with "I," the individual. Hegelian triads are also evident in the division of the work into chapters and sections.

But again, as in Hegel, it appears that the divisions are

194 Mackay, *Max Stirners kleinere Schriften*, pp. 85-102.
195 The English translation of *Der Einzige und sein Eigenthum* has been made the basis of this discussion: *Max Stirner, The Ego and His Own: The Case of the Individual Against Authority*, trans. Steven T. Byington; ed., with annotations and an introduction, by James J. Martin (New York: Libertarian Book Club, 1963).
196 McLellan, *The Young Hegelians and Karl Marx*, p. 119.
197 *Ibid.*, p. 120.

superimposed on the text, rather than indicating a pattern of development. The entire book, from beginning to end, constitutes what one commentator calls "a self-consistent, seamless unity."[198] It even begins and ends with the same words. Another commentator describes the structure thus:

> If one searches in vain for a rectilean development, one is all the more surprised to find an extremely rigorous concentric development. If the ideas do not succeed each other according to a determinate logical order, they are nevertheless ceaselessly deepening as they unfold. The same ideas return at later stages, enriched in meaning.[199]

Stirner takes up the same topics time after time: Christianity, communism, capitalism, humanity, etc. Each time he returns to a topic, he examines it from a slightly different point of view. The effect is cumulative; Stirner's argument becomes better understood as it goes through these cycles. To remove any of his passages on a given topic from its context in the book is to give the impression of a master of epigram, but not of a deep thinker. To gather all his passages on a given topic together and quote them one after the other would probably give the impression of one who harps on the same idea *ad nauseam*. But if the work is read as Stirner wrote it, the reader finds himself carried along a spiral road, inexorably down, down from the heights of God, Humanity, Love, Morality, and Truth, to the isolated, atomistic, egoistic *Einzige*, or "Unique One." "The Unique One" is, indeed, the title of the last chapter of the book; but the idea has been present from the beginning, coming and going, and growing more and more familiar with each appearance.

Another Hegelian aspect of Stirner's procedure is the "careful

---

198 Paterson, *The Nihilistic Egoist: Max Stirner*, p. 62.

199 Henri Arvon, *Aux sources de l'existentialisme: Max Stirner* (Paris: Presses Universitaires de France, 1954), quoted by Paterson, *The Nihilistic Egoist: Max Stirner*, p. 62.

attention paid to the language and the roots of words."[200] While Hegel found the German language to have a "speculative tendency" because of the presence in it of words with opposed meanings, Stirner frequently uses nuances of meaning of the same or related words to suggest connections in his argument: "The thread of thought is carried on largely by the repetition of the same word in a modified form of sense."[201] Although Stirner seems to have been a fair linguist (his translator, a philologist, finds little to quarrel with in his etymologies), he usually does not base an entire argument on a supposed derivation of words. And even when he explicitly does do this,[202] his contention does not stand or fall with the validity of his etymology, since he brings in numerous other arguments to the same conclusion. Most of the time, his plays on words are merely suggestive, meant to provoke thought, but not to establish any conclusion; for example, he asserts that by individual violence, or as it is called, "crime" (*Verbrechen*), the state's violence is "overcome" (*brechen*).[203] Thus, while Stirner's style suffers somewhat in translation, his thought probably loses as little as that of any thinker when read in a language not his own.

The foregoing related to the structure of Stirner's book and his style. His actual philosophical method turns out to be very Hegelian: the triad (affirmation, negation, and negation of negation, resulting in the transcendence and synthesis of the two former positions), is in evidence throughout the book. Stirner's main theme is the dialectic between the corporeal, the spiritual, and their *Aufhebung*, the individual or Unique One (*der Einzige*). Frequently, the dialectic in Stirner never passes beyond

---

200 McLellan, *The Young Hegelians and Karl Marx*, p. 118.

201 Stirner, *The Ego and His Own*, Translator's Introduction, p. xxi.

202 The most glaring case is where he relates *Gesellschaft* (society) to its origin, *Sal* (hall), and goes on to argue from this to the impersonal nature of society, pp. 217-218. I have noticed only a few other instances of this practice.

203 Stirner, *The Ego and His Own*, p. 197.

Max Stirner Versus Karl Marx

the first two stages, in which one position is revealed as its opposite; then it becomes and ironic method, akin to that in Hegel's *Phenomenology*, in which one attitude or position is seen to be, on close inspection, identical with its opposite.

For Stirner, as for Hegel, the dialectic is not a procedure the philosopher superimposes upon his material, but a pattern to be observed in reality itself. This does not imply that reality is wholly spiritual for Stirner; indeed, it is one of his objectives to refute this notion. According to Stirner, the dialectical movement occurs only in that part of reality which *is* spiritual: the minds of men. It does not seem to occur in matter.

3. The *Ego and His Own*: Argument

Given the peculiar, "seamless," concentric style of The Ego and His Own, the problem of how to present its arguments is a serious one. It is difficult to separate Stirner's points from his manner of expressing them. The best method would be to duplicate Stirner's involuted style; but either a great deal would have to be left out and the goal of a faithful account would be missed; or the exposition would be nearly as long as Stirner's original, and would be superfluous. Spinoza's thought probably gains in clearness and credibility, at least for modern readers, by being detached from its rigid, geometrical manner of presentation; but the same is not true of Stirner's thought.

Nevertheless, the only practicable procedure here seems to be to force Stirner's thought into something more like a straightforward, linear pattern of development, presenting his comments on each issue together, and the issues in succession, in an approximation to a deductive order.

Stirner's theme is the Hegelian (and Young-Hegelian) concept of alienation; he does not refer to it by that name, but reveals it through examples. Alienation is the self-division of man into two parts, one of which he allows to dominate him. Man is basically body and mind(*Geist*); in the modern period, it is his mind that dominates, by means of its creations in fictions, such as God, Humanity, the state, society, morality, etc. By subjecting these fictions to analysis, Stirner hopes to *show*—rather than prove—that they are unreal, and thereby reduce mind to its real status as an aspect of an; man is more than body *or* mind: he is the negative unity, or *Aufhebung*, of both. He is the *Unique One*, and they are his property, to use as he pleases—he is not to be used by them. Stirner's basic message is an individual one; it is, as Herbert Read says, "a plea for the integration of the personality."[204] But in the course of this message—intermixed with it in his peculiar, periodic style—Stirner enters, in a critical way, into the realm of social and political philosophy: he attacks the general idea of government, as well as three forms of liberalism then current; but he gives only enigmatic hints as to the positive social theory with which he would replace them.

Stirner was writing for a particular audience and this makes his book both a product of its time, and at the same time extremely relevant today. The work is given a parochial tone by the fact that it is a dialogue with a group of men who made up a small minority of the intelligentsia of the period. The vast majority of their countrymen were devout Christians and loyal subjects of the monarch; but this group was, by and large, atheistic and politically radical. Stirner is writing to and against this latter group; his quarrels with them are intramural quarrels, carried on in their peculiar parlance, and dealing with their issues. In this sense, the work is very much a product of one small aspect of its time.

But for the same reason, it is very relevant today. Like all the Young Hegelians, and like Hegel himself, Stirner saw himself as standing at the gateway to a new era: he thought that it was to be an age of egoism, and he its prophet. He was wrong in his characterization; the new age belongs to his intellectual opponents, the "liberals" (including communism under the head of "liberalism," as Stirner himself did). In his critique of the ideas of

---

204 Read, *The Tenth Muse*, p. 80.

his contemporaries, then, Stirner is criticizing the very bases of modern social and political thought.

The Ego and His Own opens with a short prologue, which encapsules the basic message of the book in a dialectical analysis of the concept of self-sacrifice, showing that it really implies egoism. This prologue is headed by the motto *Ich hab' Mein Sach' auf Nichts gestellt*,[205] from a poem by Goethe: literally, this means "I have based my cause on nothing" (Byington translates is as "All things are nothing to me," which has the same sense). These are also the last words of the book. In the prologue, Stirner examines the various causes we are exhorted to sacrifice our interests to serve:

> The Good Cause, then God's Cause, the cause of mankind, of truth, of freedom, of humanity, of justice; further, the cause of my people, my prince, my fatherland; finally, even the cause of Mind, and a thousand other causes. Only *my* cause is never to be my concern. "Shame on the egoist who thinks only of himself!"[206]

He then asks whether these being sacrifice for anything beyond themselves; of course, they do not. God serves the cause of truth and love, but these are identical with His essence, and so He really serves only Himself. "His cause is—a purely egoistic cause." The same is true of mankind, truth, freedom, justice, the nation, all of which serve only themselves, while simultaneously being served by millions of people. The other side of self-sacrifice, then, is egoism. Stirner proposes to "take a lesson" from "those great egoists," and instead of unselfishly serving them, "rather to be the egoist myself." He summarizes his conclusion:

---

205 Stirner, *The Ego and His Own*, p. 3.

206 *Ibid.* There is an immediate paradox here in German, as "cause" and "concern" are the same word: *Sache*. Thus the sentence could be rendered, "Only my cause is never to be my cause"—a self-contradiction.

The divine is God's concern; the human man's. My concern is neither the divine nor the human, not the true, good, just, free, etc., but solely what is mine, and it is not a general one, but is—unique[*einzig*], as I am unique.

Nothing is more to me than myself![207]

Stirner does not believe that these entities really exist in a personal form that would allow them to be either egoists or altruists; the rest of his book is an attempt to show how these being, which are really nothing but our own ideas, come to be reified and to exact tribute from us.

In order to account for this reification of the ideal, Stirner embarks on several dialectical account of history. The first is a personal history, a purported description of the growth and intellectual development of a single human being from childhood to adulthood; he then goes on to show that the progress of human civilization has followed the same course.

The ostensible purpose of the various accounts is to indicate the process whereby the contemporary world arrived at its condition of alienation; in other words, much the same purpose as Hegel's in *The Philosophy of History*. What counts, however, is the accuracy of the description of the present, which could still remain true even if the historical interpretation were rejected. If modern man *is* suffering from alienation, it does not matter much how he got that way; although grasping the process whereby this occurred (even if not the actual process) will aid in understanding this condition.

Two of the three accounts will be telescoped here. The three stages of the individual life are childhood, youth, and manhood. Corresponding to childhood in the world history are (in the first account) the ancient world and (in the second account) the period of "negroidity." Corresponding to the stage of youth are, respectively, "the Moderns," encompassing the Christian period

---

207 *Ibid.*, p. 5.

and including (Stirner's) present, and the period of "mongoloid-ity." Manhood is the time of the future; in the first account, it will be the age of the egoist; in the second, that of the Caucasian. The triad negroid-mongoloid-caucasian will be omitted from consideration here; it does not add materially to the argument.

The first period is the time of realism: the child is concerned with things external to him, including his parents; as in the Phenomenology (though there, only in the encounter of two self-consciousnesses), there is an unavoidable "combat of self-assertion," in which the "victor become the lord, the vanquished one the subject." The child's method of fighting is to "get at what is 'back of' things," to "spy out the weak points of everybody." The child discovers that back of, and mightier than, the commands and punishments of its parents are its own courage and shrewdness; in other words, its own mind (*Geist*; here "mind" seems a better translation than "spirit.")[208]

The same conquest of the world through the power of the mind is exemplified in classical antiquity. The ancients, like the child, are bound up with the world; their wisdom is directed toward mastering the world, not toward escaping from it. Such worldly, natural considerations as the soil of the fatherland, blood relations, and funeral rites constitute an absolute truth for them.

The process of liberation from the world begins with the Sophists: "They recognize in *mind* man's true weapon against the world."[209] The understanding was now free from and could be turned against the world. But another part of the mind—the "heart"—was still ruled by the natural impulses and appetites; unless it were purified, "then it was unavoidable that the free understanding must serve the 'bad heart.'" It was Socrates, "the founder of ethics," who began this purging of the heart.[210] This was carried to a higher degree by the Stoics and Epicureans, but theirs were still "practical philosophies," means of dealing with the world:

---

208 *Ibid.*, pp. 9-10.
209 *Ibid.*, p. 17.
210 *Ibid.*

the Stoics by repelling the world, the Epicureans by deceiving it. The complete break with the world is achieved by the Skeptics, who find no truth in the world at all. Mind or spirit is now all in all, and the stage is set for the transition to Christianity.[211]

The second stage of the individual's development is that of adolescence or youth, in which the newly-discovered mind is made the center of attention; the youth retreats completely into the sphere of mind, and regards material things as manifestations of abstract concepts. He "does not try to get ahold of *things* (for instance, to get into his head the *data* of history), but the *thoughts* that lie hidden in things, and so, therefore, of the *spirit* of history."[212] But the youth begins to compare objects with his thoughts about them and to see that the former fall short of the latter; thus he turns back to the world, "everywhere fancying it amiss and wanting to improve it,"[213] to make it correspond to his ideals of "truth, freedom, humanity, Man," and so on.

The corresponding stage of Western history is the period of "the Moderns," the Christian period. It is an age dominated by religion in many forms, with Christianity the prototypical religion: its concern is wholly with the spirit and things of the spirit.

The Christian period has gone through two major stages, the Middle Ages and the post-Reformation period. Common to both is "hierarchy," the "dominion of thoughts, dominion of mind."[214] He also refers to this phenomenon as "possession by spirits,[215] and, more literally, as insanity:

> Do not think that I am jesting or speaking figuratively when I regard those persons who cling to the Higher, and (because the vast majority belongs under this head) almost the whole world of men, as veritable fools, fools

---

211 *Ibid.*
212 *Ibid.*
213 *Ibid.*, p. 12.
214 *Ibid.*, p. 74.
215 *Ibid.*, p. 34.

in a madhouse. What is it, then, that is called a "fixed idea"? An idea that has subjected to man to itself. When you recognize, with regard to such a fixed idea, that it is a folly, you shut its slave up in an asylum....Is not all the stupid chatter of most of our newspapers the babble of fools who suffer from the fixed ideas of morality, legality, Christianity, and so forth, and only seem to go about free because the madhouse in which they walk takes in so broad a space? Touch the fixed idea of such a fool, and you will at once have to guard your back against the lunatic's stealthy malice. For these great lunatics are like the little so-called lunatics in this point too—that they assail by stealth him who touches their fixed idea. They first steal his weapon, steal free speech from him, and then fall upon him with their nails.[216]

The change from the pre- to the post-Reformation period has been the increased severity of this dominion of ideas over men. The "fixed idea" of the Middle Ages was that of God, who was separate from the individual and his physical world; the individual was related to God only through the intermediaries of priest, saints, etc. But Protestantism brings the individual into direct relationship to the divine; every man his own priest.

> Protestantism has actually put a man in the position of a country governed by secret police. The spy and the eavesdropper, "conscience," watches over every motion of the mind, and all thought and action is for it a "matter of conscience," that is, police business. This tearing apart of man into "natural impulse" and "conscience" (inner populace and inner police) is what constitutes the Protestant.[217]

---

216 *Ibid.*, p. 43.
217 *Ibid.*, p. 89.

Even among those who consider themselves liberated from superstitious dogma, the characteristic religious phenomenon is to be found: the sense of the "sacred." Here it is morality which constitutes the fixed idea:

> Take notice how a "moral man" behaves, who today often thinks he is through with God and throws off Christianity as a bygone thing. If you ask him whether he has ever doubted that the copulation of brother and sister is incest, that monogamy is the truth of marriage, that filial piety is a sacred duty, then a moral shudder will come over him at the conception of one's being allowed to touch his sister as wife also. And whence this shudder? Because he *believes* in those moral commandments. This moral *faith* is deeply rooted in his breast. Much as he rages against the *pious* Christians, he himself has nevertheless as thoroughly remained a Christian—to wit, a *moral* Christian.[218]

The increased domination of the spiritual is also manifest in the political sphere. The actual ruler has been replaced by the spiritual conception of the law, which is even more binding: "They only changed the *existing* objects, the real ruled, into *conceived* objects, into *ideas*, before which the old respect not only was not lost, but increased in intensity."[219]

We see here, then, the same dialectical movement as in the individual biography: in the first stage, the movement is away from the world into mind; in the second, the movement is to bring the world itself into the realm of the mind, to make it more like the mental ideals, by improving it, "spiritualizing" it, "hallowing" it.

Stirner sees the climax of this movement in the Young Hegelians, of whom Feuerbach has presumably gone the farthest in freeing men from the domination of religion. For Stirner,

---

218 *Ibid.*, pp. 46-47
219 *Ibid.*, p. 87.

Feuerbach is the epitome of the religious thinker: he has abolished all separation between man and God, and placed God *within* man himself, in the form of the "human essence." Here He is all the more inescapable.[220] Feuerbach is not, as he thinks, abolishing Christianity, but rather increasing its hold over us.[221] This is "the HUMAN religion," which "separates my essence from me and sets it above me,...exalts 'Man' to the same extent as any other religion does its God or idol," and "thereby creates for me a 'vocation,'"[222] namely, to approximate myself to this perfect essence in my actual life. This human religion Stirner also designates "liberalism," and its exponents include most of the other Young Hegelians. In the course of the book, Stirner criticizes Bruno and Edgar Bauer, Hess, Wilhelm Weitling, Marx,[223] and others as liberals. All of them have in common the tendency to divide man into an essential and unessential aspect, and demand that the whole man live up to his essence.

In liberalism, people relate to each other not as individuals, but as exemplifications of "essence." This means that individuals can be sacrificed in the name of the ideal. The liberals recognized that religion divides men along sectarian lines, and opposed it for that reason. But liberalism does exactly the same thing: it loves men only insofar as they reveal the human essence, not for what they are as individuals.

> Get away from me with your "philanthropy"! Creep in, you philanthropist, into the "dens of vice," linger awhile in the throng of the great city: will you not everywhere find sin, and sin, and again sin? Will you see a rich man without finding him pitiless and "egoistic"? Perhaps you already call yourself an atheist, but you remain true to the Christian feeling that a camel will sooner go through

---

220 *Ibid.*, p. 48.
221 *Ibid.*, p. 32.
222 *Ibid.*, p. 176.
223 *Ibid.*

a needle's eye than a rich man not be an "un-man." How many do you see anyhow that you would not throw into the "egoistic mass"? What, therefore, has your philanthropy (love of man) found? Nothing but unlovable men![224]

Corresponding to this modern liberal "religion," Stirner finds three characteristic political philosophies, which he calls "political," "social," and "human liberalism." This last is the peculiar theory of Bruno and Edgar Bauer and their followers, and will be neglected here. Political liberalism is the theoretical basis of the modern bourgeois state. By "social liberalism," Stirner understands the theories of the communists. He is here evaluating the modern world almost at its moment of birth.

Political liberalism has its roots in the struggle of the bourgeoisie against the privileged classes. The bourgeoisie called for equality of all citizens of the state; persons were no longer to be respected on the basis of birth or position. Stirner paraphrases their battle cry:

> No more distinction, no giving preference to persons, no difference of classes! Let all be alike! No separate interest is to be pursued longer, but general interest of all. The State is to be a fellowship of free and equal men, and everyone is to devote himself to the "welfare of the whole," to be dissolved into the State, to make the state his end and ideal.[225]

What has, in fact, happened is the replacement of the old privileged classes by the bourgeoisie, made possible by the egalitarian political slogans; the difference is that not the bourgeoisie is called the "nation."[226] They made themselves the representa-

---

224 *Ibid.*, p. 360.
225 *Ibid.*, p. 99.
226 *Ibid.*, p. 101.

Max Stirner Versus Karl Marx

tives of the universal, and so increased their power manifold over that of the feudal ruler:

> The monarch in the person of the "royal master" had been a paltry monarch compared with this new monarch, the "sovereign nation." This *monarchy* was a thousand times severer, stricter, and more consistent. Against the new monarch there was no longer any right, any privilege at all; how limited the "absolute king" of the *ancien régime* looks in comparison! The Revolution effected the transformation of *limited monarchy* into *absolute monarchy*. From this time on every right that is not conferred by this monarch is an "assumption"; but every prerogative that he bestows a "right." The times demanded *absolute royalty*, absolute monarchy; therefore down fell that so-called absolute royalty which had so little understood how to become absolute that it remained limited by a thousand little lords.[227]

This is, however, the state demanded by the German bourgeois liberals; it is supposed to be freer than the feudal state, in which individuals were subjected to other individuals rather than to "impersonal" laws. This leads Stirner to his definition of "liberty" as exemplified in liberalism: it is never the freedom of the individual that is increased, but the freedom of that which enslaves him:

> Political liberty means that the *polis*, the State, is free; freedom of religion that religion is free, and freedom of conscience signifies that conscience is free; not, therefore, that I am free from the State, from religion, from conscience, or that I am *rid* of them. It does not mean my liberty, but the liberty of a power that rules and

---

227 *Ibid.*, p. 102.

subjugates me; it means that one of my *despots*, like State, religion, conscience, is free.[228]

The slavery in the bourgeois-liberal state, however, is unequal: "If an age is imbued with an error, some always derive advantage from the error, while the rest have to suffer from it."[229] In this state, the bourgeois class benefits; the state protects its property and allows it to exploit the labor of the proletariat:

> The State pays well that is "good citizens," the possessors, may be able to pay badly without danger; it secures to itself by good payment its servants, out of whom it forms a protecting power, a "police" (to the police belong soldiers, officials of all kinds, those of justice, education, etc.—in short, the whole "machinery of the State") for the "good citizens," and the "good citizens" gladly pay high tax-rates to it in order to pay so much lower rates to their laborers.[230]

This anomaly of political liberalism is recognized by the social liberals, that is, the socialists or communists. They see, says Stirner, that the desired equality has not been achieved, since "even if the persons have become equal, yet their possessions have not."[231] The social liberal reasons as follows:

> He now asks himself further, are we to let what we rightly buried come to life again? Are we to let this circuitously restored inequality of persons come to pass? No; on the contrary, we must bring quite to an end what was only half accomplished. Our freedom from another's person still lacks the freedom from what the other's person can

---

228 *Ibid.*, p. 107.
229 *Ibid.*, p. 114.
230 *Ibid.*, p. 115.
231 *Ibid.*, p. 116.

command, from what he has in his personal power—in short, from "personal property." Let us then do away with *personal property*. Let no one have anything any longer, let everyone be a—ragamuffin[*Lump*]. Let property be *impersonal*, let it belong to—*society*.[232]

The communists want to create a new order in which business fluctuations will no longer be possible. But then, like the religious people they really are, they want to make this new order "sacred." This new order is no less oppressive than any of the other idols men have erected over themselves:

> Communism, by the abolition of all personal property, only presses me back still more into dependence on another, to wit, on the generality or collectivity; and, loudly as it always attacks the "State," what it intends is itself again a State, a *status*, a condition hindering my free movement, a sovereign power over me. Communism rightly revolts against the pressure that I experience from individual proprietors; but still more horrible is the might that it puts in the hands of the collectivity.[233]

The social liberal, like all religious people, divides the individual into an essential and non-essential part:

> That the communist sees in you the man, the brother, is only the Sunday side of Communism. According to the work-day side he does not by any means take you as a man simply, but as human laborer or laboring man. The first view has in it the liberal principle; in the second, illiberality is concealed. If you were a "lazy-bones," he would not indeed fail to recognize the man in you but would endeavor to cleanse him as a "lazy man" from

---

232 *Ibid.*, p. 117.
233 *Ibid.*, p. 257.

laziness and to convert you to the *faith* that labor is man's "destiny and calling."[234]

Liberalism, like the older forms of religion, deals harshly with those who do not live up to its ideal. The essence of the individual is the true man; the rest of his traits constitute the "un-man" (*Unmensch*). Considering recent events in the Soviet Union, Stirner is prophetic when he compares political and social liberalism on this point:

> Let a State's tolerance go ever so far, toward an un-man and toward what is inhuman it ceases. And yet this "un-man" is a man, yet the "unhuman" itself is something human, yes, possible only to a man, not to any beast; it is, in fact, something "possible to man." But, although every un-man is a man, yet the State excludes him; it locks him up, or transforms him from a fellow of the State into a fellow of the prison (fellow of the lunatic asylum or hospital, according to Communism).[235]

The "modern world is "possessed" by "spooks" (*Spuk*). Individuals relate to each other not as individuals, but always through the intermediary of these spooks, or fixed ideas, which are sacred to them. They come in many varieties and Stirner deals with all of them at various points throughout the book: God, Man, Family, Truth, Freedom, Equality, Fatherland, People, and so one. These are all products of the mind; but they are believed to have an existence of their own. They dominate by making the individual dissatisfied with himself or his situation, both of which he wants to modify to accord with the idea. He will go so

---

234 *Ibid.*, p. 122.

235 *Ibid.*, p. 177. Stirner was not gifted with precognition; the communists of his time were already discussing the "rehabilitation" of recalcitrants through institutionalization. Stirner cites a passage from Weitling to this effect on p. 240.

Max Stirner Versus Karl Marx

far as to lay down his very life for this idea—e.g., the Fatherland—if called upon to do so.

To find out what Stirner would put in the place of this mass delusion, we revert to his account of human and historical development. The third stage of the individual is the man; he is the *Aufhebung* of the two preceding stages. The child was concerned with bodily things, the youth with the spiritual; the man realizes that both are merely his qualities, that he is both body and mind, and more than either.

> Therefore the man shows a *second* self-discovery. The youth found himself as spirit and lost himself again in the *general* spirit, the complete, holy spirit, Man, mankind—in short, all ideals; the man finds himself as *embodied* spirit.[236]

The man no longer deals with the world according to his ideals, seeking to reform it after the model of these ideals. Instead of this, he deals with the world according to his own "interest."[2][237] He is the egoist.

He was, however, an egoist all the time, but without knowing it. "From the moment when he catches sight of the light of the world a man seeks to find out himself and get hold of himself out of its confusion...."[238] His interest is always in himself; but when he discovers himself as mind, he gets carried away into the universal, and becomes divided against himself, or alienated. It is only as the man that he grasps his true nature as an individual, corporeal being who also possesses a mind.

This is, of course, merely a model. Stirner believes that the "men" of his own day have not reached this level; Western culture is still in its youth, with the transition to manhood, Stirner hopes, about to take place. But his contemporaries, like the hypothetical

---

236 *Ibid.*, p. 13.
237 *Ibid.*, p. 12.
238 *Ibid.*, p. 9.

youth, are still egoists without knowing it, "involuntary egoists."
Again, as in the prologue, he analyzes self-sacrifice to find egoism
implicit in it:

> Just recognize yourselves again, just recognize what
> you really are, and let go your hypocritical endeavors,
> your foolish mania to be something else than you are.
> Hypocritical I call them because you have yet remained
> egoists all these thousands of years, but sleeping, self-de-
> ceiving, crazy egoists,...you self-tormentors. Never yet
> has a a religion been able to dispense with "promises,"
> whether they referred us to the other world or to this
> ("long life," etc.); for man is a mercenary and does not
> "gratis." But how about that "doing good for the good's
> sake" without prospect of reward? As if here too the pay
> was not contained in the satisfaction that it is to afford.
> Even religion, therefore, is founded on our egoism and—
> exploits it; calculated for our *desires*, it stifles many oth-
> ers for the sake of one. This then gives the phenomenon
> of *cheated* egoism, where I satisfy, not myself, but one of
> my desires, such as the impulse towards blessedness.[239]

The involuntary egoist becomes enslaved to a part of himself.
Stirner is calling for an end to this self-division of the personality; he is advocating something like what is nowadays referred to
as "the whole man." The difference, however, is that those who
call for "the whole man" (and this includes Marx) usually have
some pattern in mind into which the individual is supposed to
fit himself. Stirner has no such pattern; each individual is unique
(*einzig*) and has only consciously to develop this individuality to
become "*der Einzige*," the Unique One.

The goal of this process of self-liberation is not, as one
might expect, freedom. To Stirner, freedom is just one more

---

239 *Ibid.*, pp. 164-165

unattainable ideal. To be free is to be "rid of" something;[240] to-tal freedom would mean being rid of everything, and this is not even desirable: "If you became free from everything, you would no longer have anything; for freedom is empty of substance."[241] But partial freedom is unsatisfactory, also: "The freer I become, the more compulsion piles up before my eyes; and the more impotent I feel myself....if I have invented railroads, I feel myself weak again because I cannot yet sail through the skies like the bird..."[242] Thus the quest for freedom becomes endless, like all other "religious" ideals.

Instead of freedom, Stirner's goal is *Eigenheit,* "personality." He uses it constantly in conjunction with *eigen,* "to own," and *Eigener,* "owner." The English translator has solved the problem by coining the word "ownness" for this locution.[243] Thus, Stirner says: "I have no objection to freedom, but I wish more than freedom for you: you should not merely be rid of what you do not want; you should not only be a 'freeman,' you should be and 'owner' too."[244]

"Ownness" is Stirner's solution to the problem of alienation. It is a recognition that the

higher being before which one has bowed down are figments of one's mind, and a reclaiming of them as one's property. Thus ownness includes freedom: "Must we then, because freedom betrays itself as a Christian ideal, give it up? No, nothing is to be lost, freedom no more than the rest; but it is to become our own, and in the form of freedom it cannot."[245] Introspection and analysis reveal that the desire for freedom really implies the notion of ownness; ownness is logically prior to freedom:

---

240 *Ibid.,* p. 157.
241 *Ibid.,* p. 156.
242 *Ibid.*
243 *Ibid.,* p. 155 n.
244 *Ibid.,* p. 156.
245 *Ibid.,* p. 157.

Philip Breed Dematteis

What have you then when you have freedom—for I will not speak here of your piecemeal bits of freedom—complete freedom? Then you are rid of everything that embarrasses you, everything, and there is probably nothing that does not once in your life embarrass you and cause you inconvenience. And for whose sake, then, did you want to be rid of it? Doubtless *for your* sake, because it is in *your* way! But if something were not inconvenient to you; if on the contrary, it were quite to your mind (such as the gently but *irresistibly commanding* look of your loved one)—then you would not want to be rid of it and free from it. Why not? For your sake again! So you take *yourselves* as measure and judge over all. You gladly let freedom go when unfreedom the "sweet service of love," suits *you*; and you take up your freedom again on occasion when it begins to suit *you* better—that is, supposing, which is not the point here, that you are not afraid of such a Repeal of the Union for other (perhaps religious) reasons.[246]

Stirner scoffs at the liberals who petition the government for freedoms of various kinds: being still possessed, they do not realize that the only real freedom is that which comes from "ownness." In other words, freedom must be taken by the individual, not granted by some power hovering over him: "My freedom becomes complete only when it is my—might; but by this I cease to be a merely free man, and become an own man."[247] Stirner gives an example of his principle in a discussion of freedom of the press, the gist of which is that even in the most liberal states, the press is only free within certain limits; as soon as it begins to endanger something "sacred," whatever that might be in a given instance, it will certainly be revoked. Stirner, therefore, demands, not freedom of the press, but "*ownness of the press* or *property* in

---

246 *Ibid.*, pp. 160-161.
247 *Ibid.*, p. 166.

the press."[248] This no government can grant; what is one's "own" is what one has to take for himself, not what he hold "in fief" from a higher power.

> If the press is *my own*, I as little need a permission of the State for employing it as I seek that permission in order to blow my nose. The press is my *property* from the moment when nothing is more to me than myself; for from this moment State, Church, people, society, and the like, cease, because they have to thank for their existence only the disrespect that I have for myself, and with the vanishing of this undervaluation they themselves are extinguished; they exist only when they are *above me*, exist only as *powers* and *power-holders*. Or can you imagine a State whose citizens one and all think nothing of it?"[249]

Stirner generalizes from this case beyond the "right" to freedom of the press: right itself is the same as might. But people believe that there is a "thing," a "spook" called "right," which somehow confers upon the possessor the ability to do something:

> You start back in fright before others, because you think you see beside them the ghost of right, which, as in the Homeric combats, seems to fight as a goddess at their side, helping them. What do you do? Do you throw your spear? No, you creep around to gain the spook over to yourselves, that it may fight on your side: you woo for the ghost's favor.[250]

Stirner does not necessarily mean by "might," physical force. "Might" simply means ability, power, capability, of whatever sort,

---

248 *Ibid.*, p. 283.
249 *Ibid.*, p. 284.
250 *Ibid.*, p. 193.

including one's reason.[251] The right to do or to have something is no more than the ability to do or to have it; if the "right" is denied by a superior power, then it does not exist, or does so only as a frustrated desire in the mind of the one who has been denied it. This position can be found in Hegel's *Philosophy of History* as applied to people: that people which assumes the ascendant position in a given epoch is in the right as against the rest, and the proof that it is in the right—that is the vehicle of the world-spirit at that time—is just the fact that it *is* in the ascendancy.

Stirner has been presented above as a critic of social theories. What is his own social theory? What organizational scheme would he set up in place of those advanced by the liberals?

Stirner's basic message is individual; he is not concerned with forecasting or with designing utopias. He is suggesting a mode of life for the individual, independent of the social circumstances. For the most part, therefore, he presupposes the existing societal and governmental framework; the "promised land" is not in the future, but can be had now, if the individual will become an "own man"—an "*Einzige*"—and take it.

For example, if he is living in a country with no freedom of the press, as Stirner himself was, he does not have to pine for the day when there will be such a "right"; nor does he have to wait until enough of the proletariat is ready to join him in a revolution which will set up a state in which this "right" will be guaranteed. If he desires freedom of the press, he has but to take it, by any means available to him, such as a clandestine press.[252] Stirner also uses the example of free trade:

> But, if I am Man, and have really found in myself him whom religious humanity designated as the distant goal, then everything "truly human" is also *my own*. What was ascribed to the idea of humanity belongs to me. That freedom of trade, for example, which humanity has yet

251 *Ibid.*, p. 188.
252 *Ibid.*, pp. 283-284.

to attain—and which, like an enchanting dream, people remove to humanity's golden future—I take by anticipation as my property, and carry it on for the time in the form of smuggling.[253]

Stirner is advocating, not the social act of revolution, but the individual act of insurrection (*Empörung*) or self-assertion:

> Revolution and insurrection must not be looked upon as synonymous. The former consists of an overturning of conditions, of the established condition or *status*, the State or society, and is accordingly a political or social act; the latter has indeed for its unavoidable consequence a transformation of circumstances, yet does not start from it but from men's discontent with themselves, is not an armed rising, but a rising of individuals, a getting up, without regard for the arrangements that spring from it. The Revolution[254] aimed at new *arrangements*; insurrection leads us no longer to *let* ourselves be arranged, but to arrange ourselves, and sets no glittering hopes on "institutions." It is not a fight against the established, since, if it prospers, the established collapses of itself; it is only a working forth of me out of the established. If I leave the established, it is dead and passes into decay. Now, as my object is not the overthrow of an established order by my elevation above it, my purpose and deed are not a political or social but (as directed towards myself and my ownness alone) an egoistic purpose and deed.[255]

Stirner remarks that in trying to think up an example "to get greater clearness," he "unexpectedly" finds himself reelecting on Jesus as the "insurgent" par excellence. Christ was born into a

---

253 *Ibid.*, pp. 327-328.
254 I.e., the French Revolution; this is taken as the prototype of revolution.
255 Stirner, *The Ego and His Own*, p. 316.

time of intense political turmoil, when conditions were ripe for revolution; "people thought they could not accuse the founder of Christianity more successfully than if they arraigned him for 'political intrigue.'" And yet "he was precisely the one who took the least part in these political doings," and advocated rendering unto Caesar. This was "because he expected no salvation from a change of *conditions*, and this whole business was indifferent to him. He was not a revolutionist, like Caesar, but an insurgent...," "for he was not carrying on any liberal or political fight against the established authorities, but wanted to walk his *own* way, untroubled about, and undisturbed by, those authorities."[256]

Stirner is saying that political slavery, like slavery to morality, religion, and so on, is always ultimately self-enslavement. Usually, the individual is not physically held captive or even threatened by the established powers; he obeys the law because he believes it in himself. No government could last more than a few moments without at least the tacit support of most of its citizens; there would not be enough police to maintain order. The "State" is really a "state of *mind*"; stop believing in it, and it is gone—for you. This does not, of course, mean that the institutions of the state—police, army, judges, congress, etc.—will instantly vanish; but these are no more than individuals possessed by the fixation from which you have just delivered yourself. These people must be dealt with, just as one must deal with any madman who takes his delusion to be reality. The difference is that one now looks out for the main change, and *uses* the establishment in order to advance his interests, rather than allowing the establishment to use him for *its* interests. Stirner would, for instance, accept the granting of freedom of the press, if it were forthcoming, "with joy; for their permission would be to me a proof that I had fooled them and started them on the road to ruin. I am not concerned for their permission, but so much the more for their folly and overthrow."[257]

---

256 *Ibid.*, pp. 316-317.
257 *Ibid.*, p. 284.

But what would happen if insurrection became universal? What would replace the existing social arrangements?

Stirner is very enigmatic on this point; he shows a Hegelian reticence about predicting the future. He has no human "essence" from which he could deduce the future conduct of man: "It will be asked, but how then will it be when the have-nots take heart? Of what sort is the settlement to be? One might as well ask that I cast a child's nativity. What a slave will do as soon as he has broken his fetters, one must—await."[258] Nevertheless, there are scattered passages in which Stirner drops hints about something called the Union (*Verein*) of Egoists. It is an open-ended concept, not worked out in detail, but a few things are clear in regard to it.

First, the Union of Egoists is not just a projection of a possible future social organization; it exists now on a smaller scale, whenever individuals gather to accomplish something that requires their combined efforts. Second, the Union is always temporary; it lasts only so long as its purpose lasts, and then it disbands. It does not demand the loyalty or allegiance of its members: "I shall find enough anyhow who *unite* with me without swearing allegiance to my flag."[259] Third, the Union is united by "intercourse" between the members; this is a relationship of whole individuals to each other. It differs, for example, from a religious fellowship, in which the members have regard only for *part* of each other, for example, only *as Christians*. They can even love one another; if so, this will be egoistic love, wherein each loves the other because it pleases him to do so. It will not be a love based on duty or obligation; in this kind of love, the individual himself is not important—the "love," as an abstract idea, is. Stirner contrasts egoistic love with "humanitarian" love:

> I love men too—not merely individuals, but every one. But I love them with the consciousness of egoism; I love them because love makes *me* happy, I love because loving

---

258 *Ibid.*, p. 260.
259 *Ibid.*, p. 236.

is natural to me, because it pleases me. I know no "commandment of love." I have a *fellow-feeling* with every feeling being, and their torment torments, their refreshment refreshes me too; I can kill them, not torture them....

You love man, therefore you torture the individual man, the egoist, your philanthropy (love of man) is the tormenting of men.[260]

As a general social organization, the Union of Egoists would appear to be a multiplication of small groups of the above kind. Stirner seems to think that if such an organization comes about, it will be through the act of the proletariat. The first stages are much on the order of labor unions:

We do not want to take from you anything, anything at all, only you are to pay better for what you want to have. What then have you? "I have an estate of a thousand acres." And I am your plowman, and will henceforth attend to your fields only or one thaler a day wages. "Then I'll take another." You won't find any, for we plowmen are no longer doing otherwise, and, if one puts in an appearance who takes less, then let him beware of us. There is the housemaid, she too is now demanding as much, and you will no longer find one below this price. "Why, then it is all over with me. Not so fast! You will doubtless take in as much as we; and, if it should not be so, we will take off so much that you shall have wherewith to live like us." "But I am accustomed to live better." We have nothing against that, but it is not our lookout; if you can clear more, go ahead. Are we to hire out under rates, that you may have a good living? The rich man always puts off the poor with the words, "What does your want concern me? See to is how you make your way through the

260 *Ibid.*, p. 291.

world; that is your affair, not mine." Well, let us let it be our affair, then, and let us not let the means that we have to realize value from ourselves be pilfered from us by the rich.[261]

The new society would not, then, be characterized by an attempt to impose an abstract ideal of equality upon human beings who are unique and different. Each small Union of Egoists would come to an understanding among its members as to the apportionment of property and services; the understanding would not be "sacred," but subject to constant change as the interests and desires of the parties involved change.

The economic arrangement of this future society are none too clear; again, Stirner refuses to prescribe. It seems, however, that competition, which Stirner associates with the bourgeois state, would be eliminated, and replaced by consumers' cooperatives:

> Finally, as regards competition once more, it has a continued existence by this very means, that all do not attend to *their* affair and come to an *understanding* with each other about it. Bread is a need of all the inhabitants of a city; therefore they might easily agree of setting up a public bakery. Instead of this they leave the furnishing of the needful to the competing bakers. Just so meat to the butchers, wine to the wine-dealers, etc.
>
> Abolishing competition is not equivalent to favoring the guild. The difference is this: In the *guild* baking, etc., is the affair of the guild-brothers; in *competition*, the affair of chance competitors; in the union, of those who require baked goods, and therefore my affair, yours, the affair of neither the guildic nor the concessionary baker, but the affair of the *united*.
>
> If *I* do not trouble myself about *my* affair, I must be

---

261 *Ibid.*, pp. 271-272.

content with what pleases others to vouchsafe me. To have bread is my affair, my wish and desire, and yet people leave that to the bakers and hope at most to obtain through their wrangling, their getting ahead of each other, their rivalry—in short, their competition—an advantage which one could not on in the case of the guild-brothers who were lodged *entirely* and *alone* in the proprietorship of the baking franchise. –What every one requires, every one should also take a hand in procuring and producing; it is *his* affair, his property, not the property of the guildic or concessionary master.[262]

It appears from this that Stirner is willing to give up the advantages of division of labor, specialization, and the market, without a very clear notion of what is to be put in their place. This might reflect mere economic naiveté on Stirner's part; but the evidence is against this. Already noted in the account of his life was the fact that he translated the economic writings of Adam Smith and J.-B. Say into German; this occurred after he wrote *The Ego and His Own*, but it is reasonable to assume that he was familiar with the works before he undertook to translate them. This supposition is supported, in the case of Smith, by Stirner's account of the demoralizing effect of the division of labor in a pin factory.[263] The example is evidently drawn from "Smith's use of pin-manufacturing in *The Wealth of Nations* to explain the division of labour."[264] Stirner was, then, aware of classical economic theory and consciously rejected its principles. Carroll also notes that

> ...his use of the term "free trade" is intended to slight its economic usage as a technical description of the relationship between tariff laws and the import of

---

262 *Ibid.*, pp. 275-276.
263 *Ibid.*, p. 120.
264 Carroll, *Max Stirner: The Ego and His Own*, p. 102 n.

commodities. He seeks to draw back such an *alienating* abstraction in the orbit of the individual; free trade, for him, refers to consumers creating their own code of intercourse, and finding the mode of consumption which suits their particular needs.[265]

Stirner agrees with Marx in seeing economic laws not as irrefragable laws of nature, but as human creations which have become dominant over their creators; they will disappear when the rest of human alienation disappears.

But Stirner is emphatically not a communist. His hostility to the state in all its forms has caused him to be characterized traditionally as an anarchist; as we saw earlier, Plekhanov even regarded him as "the father of anarchism." On the other hand, even Woodcock, who includes Stirner in his work on anarchism, admits that:

> At first sight Stirner's doctrine seems strikingly different from that of other anarchist thinkers. These tend, like Godwin, to conceive some absolute moral criterion to which man must subordinate his desires in the name of justice and reason, or, like Kropotkin, to pose some innate urge which, once authority is brought to an end, will induce men to co-operate naturally in a society governed by invisible laws of mutual aid. Stirner, on the other hand, draws near to nihilism and existentialism in his denial of all natural laws and of a common humanity; he sets forth as his ideal the egoist, the man who realizes himself in conflict with the collectivity and with other individuals, who does not shrink from the use of any means in "the war of each against all," who judges everything ruthlessly from the viewpoint of his own well-being, and who, having proclaimed his "ownness," may then enter with

---

265 *Ibid.*, p. 162 n.

like-minded individuals into a "union of egoists," without rules or regulations, for the arrangement of matters of common convenience.[266]

Nor has Stirner had more than fleeting and isolated effects upon historical anarchist action.[267]

The account of the Union of Egoists given above, however, must lead us to quality the exclusion of Stirner from the ranks of the anarchists. He shares with other anarchists and aversion to capitalism, and thinks that it can be replaced by some kind of cooperative production. These facts, plus his diatribe against all forms of authority, place him in the anarchist tradition.

On the other hand, unlike the other anarchists, Stirner is not primarily a social philosopher; his fundamental drive is not toward the setting up of a new form of social organization. He expressly disavows the intent to draw up a blueprint for any such organization, and contents himself with suggesting what the situation *might* be like *if* egoism became universal. But his basic import is directed to the existence of the individual here and now, in the current social conditions, and is a policy for taking the optimum advantage of those conditions.

Stirner could, then, be characterized as a moralist, except that such a designation would imply that he prescribes to the individual's life-style. This is incorrect: what he does is to try to expose the illusions under which men live, and to *show* an alternative life-style. The moralist's idea that the individual has a "potential" that he ought to try to actualize in his conduct is, for Stirner, just another religious phantom. He agrees with Hegel that the individual is the sum of his acts: "We are, every moment, all that we can be; and we never need be more."[268] To the egoist, or *Einzige*, all of his "properties"(*Eigenschaften*) are his "property"(*Eigenthum*): he is corporeal, spiritual, human, German, a philosopher,

266 Woodcock, *Anarchism*, pp. 94-95.
267 Carroll, *Max Stirner: The Ego and His Own*, p. 29
268 Stirner, *The Ego and His Own*, p. 359.

a worker, and many other things, all at once. No one of these is his "true essence," to the service of which he must submerge all the rest of his attributes. "It is believed that one cannot be more than man. Rather, one cannot be less!"[269] The individual is not somehow a "part" of humanity; rather, "humanity" is only one part among many—and that not the more important—of the individual. Therefore, the Unique One has no definition:

> They say of God, "Names name thee not." That holds good of me: no *concept* expresses me, nothing that is designated as my essence exhausts me; they are only names. Likewise they say of God that he is perfect and has no calling to strive after perfection. That too holds good of me alone.[270]

He is also described as the "creative nothingness," whose whole being consists in constantly using up himself and his properties, in squandering himself; no idea is allowed to become "fixed," even for the sake of "consistency."

4. Reply to Objections

The publication of The Ego and His Own caused a storm in Young Hegelian circles, and the parties he had attacked were quick to respond. The most important of these were Szeliga (a disciple of the Bauers' school of "Pure Criticism"), Feuerbach, and Hess. Stirner replied to all three in a long article in 1845.[271] The reply enabled him further to clarify and elaborate his ideas. Of the three criticisms and responses, however, only those involving Hess will be considered here: the controversy with Szeliga is of only historical interest, and the reply to Feuerbach will be

---

269 *Ibid.*, p. 133.
270 *Ibid.*, p. 366.
271 Paterson, *The Nihilistic Egoist: Max Stirner*, p. 94. Reprinted in Mackay, *Max Stirners kleinere Schriften*, pp. 111-166.

cited in the final chapter. Hess questioned Stirner's notion of the "Union of Egoists," and the latter's answer may help in clarifying the meaning of this concept:

> Perhaps at this moment children are running together under his window in the comradeship of their play; let him look at them, and he will perceive merry egoistic unions. Perhaps Hess has a friend, a sweetheart; then he may know how heart joins itself to hears, how two of them unite egoistically in order to have the enjoyment of each other, and how neither "gets worse of the bargain." Perhaps he meets a couple of close acquaintances on the street and is invited to accompany them to a wine-shop; does he go with them in order to do them an act of kindness, or does he "unite" with them because he promises himself enjoyment from it? Do they have to give him their best thanks for his "self-sacrifice", or do they know that for an hour they formed an "egoistic union" together?[272]

Here, again, it is evident that Stirner's main concern is for the present, and not for the construction of future utopias. The "Union of Egoists" is something that exists here and now, whenever two or more individuals unite for a common purpose, then go their separate ways when that purpose has been achieved. Considerations of loyalty or duty are out of place here; all that matters is mutual enjoyment and satisfaction.

5. Summary

In spite of the length of this exposition, many interesting facets of Stirner's thought have had to be omitted. I believe, however, that most of the important points have been mentioned.

---

272 Carroll, *Max Stirner: The Ego and His Own*, p. 218 n.

Stirner's basic position is that reality consists of unique individuals, universals are mental constructs. Most people, however, behave as if they thought these fictions to have an independent reality; Stirner considers this a form of insanity, a loss of touch with reality. The cure for this condition is a conceptual analysis of these ideas which will reveal their illusory character; thus cured, individuals will be able to pursue their own interests, whatever these might be, unencumbered by this universe of imaginary entities.

His criticism of "liberal" political theories, including communism, is that they are based upon abstractions: they deduce the organization of future society from some "essence" supposed to be common to all human beings. Political liberation, for Stirner, is essentially self-liberation (insurrection), as political servitude is basically self-enslavement to one's own ideas.

Stirner's goal is to become the "Unique One" or "owner," who guides his conduct according to his realistic appraisal of the situation, including his own abilities and limitations, rather than in accordance with universals and ideals which have no existence save in his mind.

Chapter III

MARXIST CRITICISMS OF STIRNER

This chapter deals with the confrontation between Marx and Stirner from the Marxist side, by discussing the criticisms Marx and Engels directed at Stirner in *The German Ideology*, along with those of a contemporary Marxist, Hans Helms. In order to place these criticisms in their context, we will first consider some of those features of Marx's position which place him in the Hegelian tradition along with Stirner. The intent is to show that their fundamental orientation is the same, and that their differing answers to the problems of human life are primarily selections of options available within Hegelianism.

1. Marxism

Any attempt at a brief characterization of Marxism is at once open to attack from numerous sides. Among the many issues to which one must be attentive is the relationship between Marx and Engels. Some Writers consider the thought of the two men virtually indistinguishable,[273] while others believe that the mech-

---

273 M. M. Bober, *Marx's Interpretation of History* (1948; 2nd ed., revised;

anistic, deterministic cast of modern Soviet "dialectical material-ism" is primarily due to the influence of Engels.[274] Examination of the works seems to support the latter position: when Marx's writings are considered, mechanism seems foreign to his thought. On the other hand, however, there is a great deal of "circumstan-tial" evidence that must not be lightly dismissed. Engels and Marx worked in intimate collaboration for nearly forty years, during which time Marx never expressed the opinion that Engels was guilty of fundamentally misinterpreting him; and Marx was notoriously careful to distinguish his own views from any that might be confused with them. Because of this close connection, Engels would seem to have the best claim to authority as to the interpretation of Marx's thought, unless Engels was simply so obtuse that he did not grasp what Marx meant. But Marx, never generous in his praise of the intellectual competence of others, evidently recognized no such deficiency in Engels. Furthermore, the work of Engels usually cited as being responsible for the mechanistic interpretation is *Anti-Dühring*; but Engels says in the forward that he read the whole manuscript to Marx, "who approved of it as a statement of their common views."[275] And in the second edition of *Capital*, Marx quotes with approval a Russian review of the book which interprets the theory along strictly deterministic, mechanistic lines.[276]

This dispute has not been settled, but it is necessary to adopt some position in regard to it, if only provisionally. The solution that seems most reasonable to me is that Marx not himself a

New York: W. W. Norton & Company, 1965), deals with the theory of historical materialism as a unit, making little or no attempt to distinguish the contributions of the two men.

274 Dupré, *The Philosophical Foundations of Marxism*, p. viii.

275 Lewis S. Feuer (ed.), *Marx and Engels: Basic Writings on Politics and Philosophy* (Garden City, N.Y.: Doubleday & Company, 1959), p. 270.

276 Dupré, *The Philosophical Foundations of Marxism*, p. 233; Karl Marx, *Capital: A Critique of Political Economy*, ed. Friedrich Engels; Vol. I, *The Process of Capitalist Production*, trans. S. Moore and Edward Aveling (Chicago: Charles H. Kerr & Company, 1909), p. 23.

mechanistic, deterministic materialist, but regarded the process of history as a dialectic called "praxis" between nature and human consciousness. Neither term of the dialectic can be reduced to the other, or the dialectical interplay will cease. But, according to Dupré, although Marx "never sacrifices the ideal term of praxis—consciousness—he defines praxis itself so exclusively in terms of a material life process that man's transcendence over nature becomes seriously jeopardized."[277] Dupré regards this as a lapse on Marx's part, making him ultimately responsible for the deterministic misinterpretation of his theory; but the nature of the dialectic is such than an identification of nature and consciousness is unavoidable. The dialectic reveals the ultimate identity of opposed concepts; thus, if it is applied to nature and consciousness, it must result in showing them to be the same. The option then becomes one of either conceiving the operation of consciousness along the lines of nature, and therefore as determined mechanistically; or of conceiving the operation of nature according to that of consciousness, and so in terms of freedom and spontaneity. Neither choice seems satisfactory, and so the fundamental ambiguity is allowed to remain, revealing itself in alternating deterministic and non-deterministic statements. Western Marxists attempt to suppress the deterministic pole of Marx's thought by foisting it on Engels and concentrating on Marx's non-deterministic statements. The tension remains in Marx, however, and is fundamental to the dialectical conception of reality.

Another dispute revolves around the question of the continuity of Marx's thought. According to one side, there is a fundamental break in Marx's thought, occurring around 1845-1846.[278] Before the break is the period of the "Young" Marx, a humanist and ethical idealist; after the break comes the "Mature" Marx, the objective, value-free founder of "historical materialism." The "real" or "significant" Marx is found in the one or the other,

---

277 Dupré, *The Philosophical Foundations of Marxism*, p. 220.
278 Louis Althusser, *For Marx*, trans. Ben Brewster (New York: Random House, 1970), pp. 256-257; Marcuse, *Reason and Revolution*, p. 295.

according to the preference of the interpreter. The other school of thought holds that there is a continuity in Marx's work, that the "Young" and "Mature" periods are phases of a whole, and reflect a change in terminology rather than in basic concepts.[279] The dispute centers in the concept of alienation, which all acknowledge to be Marx's central concern in his early period, under the influence of Feuerbach; the question is whether he abandoned the concept, or whether the concept remained, disguised in economic terminology.

Once again, there is a wealth of evidence on both sides. Marx and Engels both talk in their later writings as if Marx had made a new beginning around 1845. Engels calls the *Theses on Feuerbach* of 1845 "the first document in which is deposited the brilliant germ of new world outlook."[280] Marx says that in The German Ideology, he and Engels "settle accounts with our erstwhile philosophical conscience,"[281] completing the break with their Young Hegelian background.

But there is also testimony to the contrary from Marx himself. In the second edition of *Capital* (1873), Marx refers to his own dialectical method as Hegel's "turned right side up" so as to remove the "rational kernel" from the "mystical shell," and says that he had criticized the "mystifying side of Hegelian dialectic" nearly thirty years previously.[282] The reference is to his *Critique of Hegel's Philosophy of Right*, written in 1843. Avineri concludes from this:

Marx in his later years thus vindicated the validity and

279 Avineri, *The Social and Political Thought of Karl Marx*, p. 5; Erich Fromm, *Marx's Concept of Man* (New York: Frederick Ungar Publishing Company, 1967), pp. 69-79; Robert C. Tucker, *Philosophy and Myth in Karl Marx* (Cambridge: At the University Press, 1969), pp. 165-176; Dupré, *The Philosophical Foundations of Marxism*, pp. 172-173 n.

280 Karl Marx and Frederick Engels, *Selected Works* (2 Vols.; London: Lawrence and Wishart, 1950), II, 325.

281 *Ibid.*, I, 330.

282 Marx, *Capital*, I, 25.

significance of the *Critique* of Hegel he had written when he was twenty-five years old. Not only is there no "caesura" between the young and old Marx, but the guarantee of continuity has been supplied by Marx himself.[283]

Avineri also points out that in 1850, well after the supposed "break" in his thought, Marx wanted to publish two of his early articles from *Deutsch-Französische Jahrbücher* in an edition of his collected works, which indicates that he still thought their contents significant. Perhaps most important is the thousand-page mass of material known as the *Grundrisse*, or *Outlines of the Critique of Political Economy*, written in 1857-1858, which forms a link between Marx's early and later work. In it, Marx outlined his plan for a comprehensive work to be called *Economics*, of which only the first part, *Capital*, ever came into being. At the same time, he notes in a letter of November, 1858, that the *Grundrisse* is "the result of fifteen years of research."[284] This would take us back to 1843, well into the "early" period and shows the continuity of Marx's thought from beginning to end.[285]

The final answer to the question of the continuity of Marx's thought has by no means been given; once again, it is necessary to take a stand without being able to adduce absolute grounds for it. We will here adopt the position, for which more evidence will be presented in the discussion below, that Marx's thought is a consistent whole, with the concept of alienation central throughout.

Two aspects of Marx's thought will be presented here: first, the concept of alienation itself, and second, Marx's dialectical conception of history.

---

283 Avineri, *The Social and Political Thought of Karl Marx*, p. 40.
284 McLellan, *The Thought of Karl Marx*, p. 110.
285 *Ibid.*

2. Alienation

For Marx, as for Feuerbach, alienation is the loss of a part of the human essence; but he differs from Feuerbach in holding that this does not occur in the ideal realm of imagination, but in actual, material reality. The change is due to Marx's different conception of the essence of man. Marx, influence by Hegel's account of the master-slave relationship in *Phenomenology* and by Hegel's discussion of property in the *Philosophy of Right*, finds the essence of man in his productive activity, or labor. For Hegel, productive labor, resulting in property, constituted an external expression of the human personality; for Marx, the act of labor itself *is* the human essence:

> The animal is immediately one with its life activity, not distinct form it. The animal is *its life activity*. Man makes his life activity itself into an object of will and consciousness. He has conscious life activity. It is not a determination with which he immediately identifies. Conscious life activity distinguished man immediately from the life activity of the animal. Only thereby is he a species-being. Or rather, he is only a conscious being—that is, his own life in an object for him—since he is a species-being. Only on that account is his activity free activity. Alienated labor reverses the relationship in that man, since he is a conscious being, makes his life activity, his *essence*, only a means for his existence.[286]

If the essence of man is his labor, then, since human labor is inherently social, it follows that man is social in his very essence: "the human essence is no abstraction inherent in each single individual. In its reality it is the ensemble of social relations."[287] This is at the root of Marx's dispute with Stirner: while Stirner

---

286 Easton and Guddat, *Writings of the Young Marx*, p. 294.
287 Marx and Engels, *Selected Works*, II, 366.

Max Stirner Versus Karl Marx

maintains that there are only individuals with no essence at all, Marx claims that the essence of the existing individuals is social. Thus, for Marx men are linked together by their very nature, while for Stirner, they are inherently isolated. Marx and Stirner are, however, in agreement that there is no *static* essence of man. Stirner sees the individual as constantly in flux; for Marx, the essence of man changes as he interacts with nature to fulfill his needs: "By thus acting on the external world and changing it, he at the same time changes his own nature."[288]

Alienation occurs when the product of man's labor becomes a commodity, an object for exchange with others: in other words, it is "alienated." But whereas in Hegel property is alienated by removing one's will from it, for Marx the commodity continues to represent an objectification of the human essence. In Feuerbach God is the imaginary externalization of the essence of man, social labor:

> Alienated labor hence turns the *species-existence of man*, and also nature as his mental species-capacity, into an existence alien to him, into the *means* of his *individual existence*. It alienated his spiritual nature, his *human essence*, from his own body and likewise from nature outside him.[289]

The commodity, originally man's own creation and externalization of his being, now begins to act according to the laws of economics and to dominate him, just as Feuerbach's God and Stirner's moral ideals dominate humanity. This is the root meaning of "alienation" in Marx's work: the human essence, as embodied in an external thing, takes on a life of its own and makes the real, living men its servants. In his mature works, Marx refers to this as exemplified in capitalism, as the "fetishism of commodities."[290]

---

288 Marx, *Capital*, I, 177.
289 Easton and Guddat, *Writings of the Young Marx*, p. 295.
290 Marx, *Capital*, I, 72.

The other meaning of alienation follows from this primary one. Man is alienated from his labor; but since his labor is inherently social, he is also alienated from other men:

> A direct consequence of man's alienation from the product of his work, from his life activity, and from his species-existence, is the *alienation of man* from *man*. When man confronts himself, he confronts other men. What holds true of man's relationship to his work, to the product of his work, and to himself, also holds true of man's relationship to other men, to their labor, and the object of their labor.[291]

This separation of man from man has its phenomenal expression in the division of labor, competition, and class struggle. In the division of labor, the expression of man's essence is restricted to a single kind of product or even a small part of a single product; but this small scope is not adequate to express his essence. The worker no longer recognizes his labor as the manifestation of his nature, but is "alienated" from it in the sense that it becomes unpleasant:

> And the worker, who for twelve hours weaves, spins, drills, turns, builds, shovels, breaks stones, carries loads, etc.—does he consider this twelve hours' weaving, spinning, driving, turning, building, shoveling, stone breaking as a manifestation of his life? On the contrary, life begins for him where this activity ceases, at table, in the public house, in bed. The twelve hours' labor, on the other hand, has no meaning for him as weaving, spinning, drilling, etc., but as *earnings*, which bring him to the table, to the public house, into bed.[292]

---

291 Easton and Guddat, *Writings of the Young Marx*, p. 295.
292 Marx and Engels, *Selected Works*, I, 77.

Max Stirner Versus Karl Marx

Instead of working cooperatively to produce the products that will satisfy their common needs, men find themselves competing with each other. The inherently social nature of man is perverted and inverted into social antagonism:

> *Therefore, as labor becomes more unsatisfying, more repulsive, competition increases and wages decrease.* The worker tries to make up the amount of his wages by working more, whether by working longer hours or by producing more in one hour. Driven by want, therefore, he still further increases the evil effects of the division of labour. The result is that *the more he works the less wages he receives*, and for the simple reason that he competes to that extent with his fellow workers, hence makes them into so many competitors who offer themselves on just the same bad terms as he does himself, and that, therefore, in the last resort he *competes* with himself, with himself as a member of the working class.[293]

Competition reigns not only among workers, but among manufacturers, between buyers and sellers, and so on. Finally, there is the competition, or struggle, between the large social groups which are divided according to their relationship to the means of production. These are the classes (*Stände*), and their contest has been the motive power of the dialectic of history: "The history of all hitherto existing society is the history of class struggles."[294]

For Marx, then, man in his essence, is related to his fellow men: individuality is a perversion of the real nature of man induced by alienation. For Stirner, on the contrary, the actual nature of man is individual, and the idea of a universal essence is a product of alienation.

---

293 *Ibid.*, 95.
294 *Ibid.*, 33.

3. Historical Materialism

Marx, along with Hegel and Stirner, saw the course of history as a dialectical process, moving on contradictions and oppositions. In accordance with his conception of the essence of man as laborer or producer of material goods, Marx located the oppositions in the interaction of human consciousness with material nature. Since humanity is essentially social, this interaction is expressed in terms of the relations between groups of men and nature, not between individuals and nature, that is, the dialectic moves on the social relations of production:

> Thus the social relations within which individuals produce, the social relations of production, change, are transformed, with the change and development of the material means of production, the productive forces. The relations of production in their totality constitute what are called the social relations, society, and, specifically, a society at a definite stage of historical development, a society with a peculiar, distinctive character. Ancient society, feudal society, bourgeois society are such totalities of production relations, each of which at the same time denotes a special stage of development in the history of mankind.[295]

By "production relations"(*Produktionsverhältnisse*), Marx seems to have in mind the relations of those engaged in the productive process, based on the ownership of the means of production (land, raw materials, tools, etc.): the persons who own these are in a position of dominance with respect to those who do not. In other words, production relations are property relations. Their situation in regard to these property relations originally constitutes a group of people, a class; later, they become conscious of

---

295 *Ibid.*, 83-84.

this position, and then the class becomes a class "for itself."[296]

The entire structure of a society at a given stage of development is based upon these relation of production; the legal system, philosophies, religion, morality of the society are such as to favor the possessing class as against the class of non-possessors:

> Social relations are intimately bound up with productive forces. In acquiring new productive forces men change their mode of production, and in changing their mode of production, their manner of making a living, they change all their social relations. The windmill gives you society with the feudal lord; the steam mill, society with the industrial capitalist.
>
> The same men who establish social relations in conformity with their material productivity also produce principles, ideas, and categories conforming to their social relations.
>
> Hence these ideas, these categories are no more eternal than the relations which they express. They are *historical and transitory products.*[297]

Over time, the methods of production change; but the property relations and the superstructure of society based on these remain the same. In other words, a contradiction arises between the economic foundation of society and the legal, political, and ideological superstructure. Since the determining factor is always economic, the relations of production and their superstructure are soon altered to correspond to the new organization of the method of production. This change is a revolution; it is brought about by the subordinate class, which now becomes dominant.[298] This is a dialectical change, resulting from opposition between substructure and superstructure. As such, it obeys the "law" of

---

296 Bober, *Marx's Interpretation of History*, pp. 96-103.
297 Easton and Guddat, *Writings of the Young Marx*, pp. 480-481.
298 Marx and Engels, *Selected Works*, I, 329.

the transformation of quantity to quality: the revolution does not occur until the productive forces have reached their maximum development in the given society; at that point, both they and the society perish and give birth to a new order.[299]

Marx distinguishes four major modes of production in history—the "Asiatic, ancient, feudal, and modern bourgeois" modes.[300] The Asiatic stage is a primitive, tribal communism, in which land is held and tilled in common and the produce divided among the members of the tribe; in addition, crafts are produced for immediate consumption and for limited trading with other tribes.[301] Ultimately (by processes detailed by Engels[302] but not Marx), the land was split up into private plots, trading increased, and the transition to the ancient system of slavery was made. In the course of this period, a polarization developed between the town- and country-dwellers; after the barbarian invasion, the dominant position is taken by the country, and feudalism begins. The two major classes are now the landowners and the serfs. Eventually, however, new towns develop, and the guilds, or bourgeoisie, begin to challenge the landowners for supremacy. The feudal system dies out in England in the fourteenth century, as serfs become independent from their landlords and the guild-masters and merchants begin to hire wage labor. The feudal legal restriction, lagging behind the change in the mode of production, hamper this process. But the feudal period comes to an explosive end with the geographical discoveries of the fifteenth century, which opened new markets and increased the demand for commodities. The guild-masters and merchants, enriched by the flow of precious minerals into Europe, particularly England, become the bourgeois class; simultaneously, with the disbanding of feudal retainers and the enclosure movement, a horde of "vagabonds" is created. These vagabonds turn to stealing, but

---

299 *Ibid.*
300 *Ibid.*
301 Marx, *Capital*, I, 89.
302 Marx and Engels, *Selected Works*, II, 232-239.

are forced to work through Draconian measures, and become the proletariat.[303] This is the first stage of capitalism, designated "original accumulation."[304] At first the processes of production are much like those used by the guilds, requiring skilled labor; gradually, an elaborate specialization and division of labor sets in. At the end of the eighteenth century comes the industrial revolution, and the modern form of capitalism emerges.

It is this form of capitalism that Marx analyzes in *Capital* and other works, and whose downfall he predicts. Like Hegel, Marx has his central focus on the present. Also like Hegel, he distinguishes between the contingent appearances of that present and the inner structure, and restricts his attention to the latter. As Marcuse puts it:

> The abstractions that underlie the first volume of *Capital* (for example, that all commodities are exchanges according to their values, that external trade is excluded, etc.) put the reality so that it "conforms with its notion." This methodological procedure is in keeping with the dialectical conception. The inadequacy between existence and essence belongs to the very core of reality. If the analysis were to confine itself to the forms in which reality appears, it could not grasp the essential structure from which these forms and their inadequacy originate. Unfolding the essence of capitalism requires that provisional abstraction be made from those phenomena that might be attributed to a contingent and imperfect form of capitalism.[305]

---

303 Karl Marx and Frederick Engels, *The German Ideology* (London: Lawrence & Wishart, 1965), pp. 71-74.

304 *Ursprüngliche Akkumulation.* This is usually translated "primary accumulation," but Bober (*Marx's Interpretation of History*) points out (p. 58 n.) that Marx called it "original accumulation" in a speech delivered in English. See Marx and Engels, *Selected Works*, I, 385.

305 Marcuse, *Reason and Revolution*, pp. 304-305.

Marx's analysis of capitalism is further Hegelian in that the very existence of the analysis is taken as evidence that the state of affairs which its subject matter is on the verge of disappearing. For Marx, capitalism reached its optimum development in England after the repeal of the Corn Laws in 1846; this period of pure *laissez faire* came to an end with the enactment of the Ten Hours Act in 1850.[306] In addition, the existence of cooperative movements such as that of Owen showed that the seeds of a different form of social organization already existed.[307] Capitalism had reached the point at which all the productive forces possible to it had been developed; it was not ready to give birth to socialism. Avineri notes the similarity in orientation between Marx and Hegel in dealing with the present:

> England, having already realized the capitalist model has moved already beyond the point at which the model can serve as an adequate explication of its mode of production. This *List der Vernunft* makes the very act of writing *Das Kapital* an index to the decomposition of capitalist society. That such a treatise could be written not as a postulate of political economy but as a description of the working of a capitalist system means that historical reality has already transcended the capitalist model and is approaching new shores. The owl of Minerva, after all, spreads its wings only with the setting of dusk.[308]

The analysis of capitalist production is based on the so-called "labor theory" of value, which is common to Marx and to classical political economy; it is entirely consistent, however, with Marx's earliest speculations on the essence of man as laborer. According to this theory, the exchange value of a product depends on the minimum labor time necessary to produce it under current

---

306 Avineri, *The Social and Political Thought of Karl Marx*, p. 161.
307 Marx and Engels, *Selected Works*, I, 347-348.
308 Avineri, *The Social and Political Thought of Karl Marx*, p. 160.

conditions.[309] Labor is purchased from the worker by the capitalist at its value, which is the cost of keeping the worker and his family alive.[310] But the worker is forced to work more hours than necessary to pay for his upkeep; he thus creates more value than he uses. This extra amount is surplus value:[311] the ratio of the surplus value to the cost of labor is the rate of exploitation of labor, and this is the source of the capitalist's profit.[312] In other words, the longer the laborer works beyond the time necessary to produce goods with a value equal to his cost of living, the more he is exploited by the capitalist. This analysis has definite similarities to Hegel's discussion of freedom and slavery in terms of the amount of labor time alienated to another.[313]

Alienation has reached its apex in capitalism: the worker's product, which embodies his essence, is taken away from him and assumes a life of its own, which proceeds according to the laws of economics; this is the "fetishism of commodities." The worker can no longer fulfill himself in his work, and so turns to "biological, animal-like functions"[314] for his satisfaction, a clear indication of the dehumanizing effects of capitalism. In the later stages of capitalism, industry reaches such a scale that it cannot be financed by the investment of the individual entrepreneur, and joint-stock companies are formed. This is the "climax of alienation," as now "not only is the worker alienated from his labour; even the capitalist is alienated, in the more sophisticated form of capitalist society, from his capital."[315]

Contradiction has also reached its apogee in the capitalist mode of production: the more the worker produces (the more

---

309 Marx, *Capital*, I, 44-45; Vol. II, *The Process of Circulation of Capital*, trans. Ernest Untermann (Chicago: Charles H. Kerr & Company, 1907), pp. 156-172.

310 *Ibid.*, I, 189-191.

311 *Ibid.*, 232.

312 *Ibid.*, 239-241.

313 Cf. Marcuse, *Reason and Revolution*, p. 195.

314 Avineri, *The Social and Political Thought of Karl Marx*, p. 106.

315 *Ibid.*, p. 179.

supply increases), the less the goods are worth—therefore, the less he and his labor are worth;[316] within the factory, there is careful, rational planning and coordination, while outside, in the society at large, there is economic anarchy, with the satisfaction of wants left to change;[317] while capitalism is based on private property and individual independence, it actually increases interdependence through the division of labor, which eliminates the last vestige of individual production and self-sufficiency;[318] the productive efficiency of the capitalist mode of production makes possible for the first time the full development of human potential, but competition forces each individual to try and minimize the potentialities of everyone else.[319]

The existence of this extreme degree of contradiction guarantees that capitalism has reached the level of development at which it is about to be *aufgehoben*. Phenomenally, the breakdown of capitalism will be manifested in a series of crises which finally make conditions unbearable, and lead to revolution on the part of the proletariat. Competition among firms will drive the less efficient out of business, leaving their assets and markets to be taken over by larger ones; thus monopolies will be formed.[320] The monopolistic firms will be more efficient, meaning that they will reduce their investment in labor in comparison to their investment in machinery, raw materials, land, and so forth. But the source of profit to the capitalist is the surplus labor provided by the worker; thus, as the ration of labor to other forms of capital declines, the rate of surplus value declines, and, with it, the rate of profit (machines cannot be exploited; they reproduce only their own value). This falling rate of profit "blunts the incentive of the capitalist,"[321] which is the whole driving force of capitalist

---

316 Easton and Guddat, *Writings of the Young Marx*, p. 289.
317 Marx, *Capital*, I, 391.
318 Avineri, *The Social and Political Thought of Karl Marx*, p. 172.
319 *Ibid.*, p. 122.
320 Marx, *Capital*, I, 685-689.
321 Bober, *Marx's Interpretation of History*, p. 223; Marx, Capital, Vol. III:

production. Aggravating this problem is overproduction: concentration and accumulation of capital lead to increased production of consumer goods; the proletariat is too poor to buy all of these, and the bourgeoisie invest their savings in new capital rather than spend them on personal consumption; the unsold goods create a glut and prices drop drastically, again leading to a lessening of incentive.[322] (We have already seen the basic outline of this process in Hegel's *Philosophy of Right*.) The depressions resulting from these conditions are followed by upturns of business activity prompted by various factors,[323] among them the opening of foreign markets[324] (again, as noted by Hegel); but these expedients are only temporary, and colonization ultimately serves only to spread the capitalist system world-wide, thereby increasing the scope of its contradictions and hastening its final demise.[325] In the course of these cycles, more and more of the landlord and middle classes are expropriated and fall into the proletariat class, leading to a society with only two classes facing each other: the small number of bourgeoisie and the masses of proletarians.[326] As the demand for labor decreases with increasing efficiency, a large pool of unemployed develops; competition for employment increases, and wage rates are pushed down while working hours go up.[327] Thus the laborers' standard of living is reduced, while they are increasingly subjected to the monotony of newer, more efficient machines on the job.[328]

The end of the capitalist, as of all the previous modes of production, will come through a revolution; but while all earlier revolutions have replaced on dominant class with another, the

---

The Process of Capitalist Production as a Whole, trans. Ernest Untermann (Chicago: Charles H. Kerr & Company, 1909), 304.

322 Marx, *Capital*, III, 568.

323 *Ibid.*, 296-299.

324 *Ibid.*, 278-279.

325 *Ibid.*, 389-391.

326 Marx and Engels, *Selected Works*, I, 39-40.

327 Marx, *Capital*, I, 689-694.

328 Marx and Engels, *Selected Works*, I, 39.

coming revolution will end class-divisions completely. In previous revolutions, the rising class always claimed to be the "universal" class, the representative of the interests of all members of the society, and in fact, it was this at the time as it was the necessary instrument of the transition to the next stage.[329] (The classes are thus an adaptation on a smaller scale of Hegel's "world-historical nations," each of which advances the development of the *Weltgeist* for a time and then makes way for the next.) But the proletariat is the truly universal class: there are no classes beneath it for it to exploit when it comes to power, and its interests are identical with those of humanity as a whole. The proletariat can only liberate itself by eliminating classes altogether, and thereby liberating all mankind.[330]

The tension in Marx's thought between free will and determinism comes out most clearly in his account of revolution. On the one hand, the revolution is necessary, guaranteed by the dialectical movement of history; on the other hand, it takes place only through the conscious action of the proletariat, who have come to a realization of the true nature of reality.[331] The consciousness of the proletariat is determined, like all consciousness, by the material conditions of the production; but this is not a "false" or "ideological" consciousness, because it (with the help of intellectual leaders, such as Marx) sees the material conditions as they really are.

Marx's account of the revolution is marked by a Hegelian reticence in predicting the future. The fact of the revolution is certain, but the exact time and manner are left open by Marx. In countries where the proletariat is in the majority, universal suffrage will allow it to come to power through the ballot;[332] in

---

329 Marx and Engels, *The German Ideology*, pp. 62-63.
330 Easton and Guddat, *Writings of the Young Marx*, pp. 262-263.
331 Marcuse, *Reason and Revolution*, pp. 317-319.
332 Karl Marx, "The Chartists," *New York Daily Tribune*, August 25, 1852; quoted by Avineri, *The Social and Political Philosophy of Karl Marx*, p. 214.

other places, force may be required.[333] Even the question of indemnity for the expropriated bourgeoisie is left open.[334] Marx thought it was possible for Russia to omit the capitalist stage entirely and progress from feudalism to a communism based on the Russian village commune (*mir*).[335]

Marx is even more reticent about the organization of future society. He indicates that there will be two post-revolutionary stages. The first is called at different times "crude communism"[336] and "socialism": during this stage, the proletariat takes over the machinery of the state and uses it to convert private into public property through nationalization, inheritance taxes, and so forth; workers now work for the government rather than for private individuals.[337] As man overcomes his alienation and regains his true, social essence, the external forms of government power will become superfluous. Engels refers to this as the "withering away" (*Abstirbung*) of the stage; Marx, however, uses the Hegelian term *Aufhebung*.[338] The state is not abolished; rather the Hegelian idea of the state as the social organism, as the true universal community of men, is taken out of its separation from the economic order of society. The individualistic civil society and its antithesis, the universalistic state, are negated and synthesized in the communist order of society. Production of goods will no longer be directed by impersonal economic forces, which are merely theoretical formulations of the alienated condition of labor, but by self-conscious choice. The anarchy of capitalist production and distribution will be replaced by cooperation in the society as a whole, thus assuring a coincidence of supply and demand; each person will be able to draw from the common storehouse to supply his needs. The economics of scarcity will be at an

---

333 Marx, *Capital*, I, 14; Bober, *Marx's Interpretation of History*, pp. 264-265.
334 Bober, *Marx's Interpretation of History*, p. 265.
335 *Ibid.*, p. 42; Feuer, *Marx and Engels: Basic Writings*, pp. 439-441.
336 Easton and Guddat, *Writings of the Young Marx*, p. 303.
337 Marx and Engels, *Selected Works*, I, 50-51.
338 Avineri, *The Social and Political Philosophy of Karl Marx*, pp. 202-302.

end; by utilizing the techniques and machinery of capitalism, the most efficient mode of production heretofore, but in a rational, unalienated manner, the society will assure itself of abundance. Most important, man will be reunited with his essence and will find satisfaction and fulfilment in his labor.[339]

This account of Marx's conception of historical development was necessarily brief, and much of the importance had to be omitted. It was, however, an essential preface to the following section, which deals with Marx's confrontation with Stirner.

4. Criticisms of Stirner: The German Ideology

The *locus* of Marx's criticism of Stirner is *The German Ideology* of 1845-1846. It is an important work in the development of Marxism, as it is the first full explanation of historical material-ism.[340] The whole work "was originally conceived as a refutation of Max Stirner's... *The Ego and His Own*,"[341] and the largest part of the book—almost four hundred pages in the English transla-tion—is devoted to this task. In addition, there are chapters of Feuerbach, Bruno Bauer, and others (although the chapter titled "Feuerbach" is primarily given over to the exposition of the ma-terialist view of history, and Feuerbach himself is scarcely men-tioned, as Engels later admitted).[342]

The criticism of Stirner takes the form of a detailed, almost line-by-line commentary on his book, which runs to a greater length than that work itself. This material is not well known, for three main reasons. First, as Dupré notes, "The first part, entitled 'Feuerbach' although only a few pages refer to him, is by far the

---

339 Marx and Engels, *Selected Works*, II, 23.
340 According to Marx's own testimony: Marx and Engels, *Selected Works*, I, 330.
341 Dupré, *The Philosophical Foundations of Marxism*, pp. 145-146.
342 Marx and Engels, *Selected Works*, II, 325.

most important,"[343] due to the elaboration there of the historical materialist theory. Second, as Hook points out, as "a running commentary upon Stirner's book," it is almost "unintelligible unless read together with Stirner's text,"[344] and Stirner's text is, as Dupré puts it, "almost forgotten."[345] Third, and perhaps most responsible for the neglect of this part of the work, is the fact that it is extremely difficult to read. McLellan goes so far as to say that it is "too turgid to be worthwhile reading."[346] Paterson very accurately describes the style, and gives an overall view of the content, in the following passage:

> Throughout the hundreds of pages of "Saint Max", Marx pursues Stirner with a savagery and rancor which, master of invective as he was, he rarely ever equaled. Every resource of sarcasm, every possibility of ridicule, is enlisted to stage this protracted parody of a world-outlook which Marx plainly considered to be literally a tissue of unpleasant fantasies, inherently grotesque but also potentially dangerous. Stirner's dreams of metaphysical conquest are brutally and tirelessly burlesqued. When Marx wearies of portraying him as "the blessed Max", whose "sacred book fell down from heaven towards the end of 1844", he casts him in the part of a modern Don Quixote, whose heroic fight against all the moral, social, and religious powers which seek to enslave him is in sad reality no more than a tilting against windmills; when this role is eventually allotted to someone else, Stirner is decked in the guise of Sancho Panze, and as "Saint Sancho" his every footstep is dogged by the relentless

343 Dupré, *The Philosophical Foundations of Marxism*, p. 146.
344 Hook, *From Hegel to Marx*, p. 173.
345 Dupré, *The Philosophical Foundations of Marxism*, p. 146.
346 McLellan, *The Young Hegelians and Karl Marx*, p. 135. He also describes it as a "long and wearisome attack...relieved by only occasional bright spots"(p. 134).

Philip Breed Dematteis

Marx, whose heavy mockery fails to conceal his real and continuous anxiety lest his prey should finally prove invulnerable to his envenomed barbs. As Marx's onslaught becomes more ferocious, the humour becomes more and more thin, what started out as a pleasing stylistic whimsy becomes a clumsy and pedantic artifice, and at the end the reader experiences a sense of incredulous relief that the monomaniac prolixity is at last over.[347]

(Possible reasons for Marx's "anxiety" will be discussed in the next chapter.)

It is impossible to deal with all of Marx's criticisms of Stirner here. Many of the attacks deal with minor points, and there is much repetition. Therefore, I shall consider only the most significant of the criticisms.

The overarching criticism which Marx directs at Stirner is that the latter is a "religious thinker." The very title of this section of the book—"Saint Max"—is part of this criticism; it is grouped with the chapter on "Saint Bruno" Bauer under the heading, "The Leipzig Council" (referring to the place of publication of the works of Bauer and Stirner).[348] *The Ego and His Own* is called "the Book," and the two Parts are designated "the Old Testament" and "the New Testament." Such a characterization of his philosophy would be particularly offensive to Stirner, since *The Ego and His Own* was an attack on just this kind of thinking. Marx is dealing with Stirner in the same way the latter dealt with Feuerbach: he is turning Stirner's own criticisms against him and revealing him as a victim of the illusions he sought to dispel in others. For Stirner, "religious" thinking was that which was concerned only with ideas; Stirner is religious in this same sense, according to

---

347 Paterson, *The Nihilistic Egoist: Max Stirner*, pp. 106-107. Paterson omits the other nickname bestowed upon Stirner by Marx: "*Jacques le bonhomme*"(Jack the Simpleton, the nickname of the French peasant). Marx and Engels, *The German Ideology*, p. 141.
348 Marx and Engels, *The German Ideology*, p. 684, n. 12.

Marx, and therefore is one more in the long line of philosophers who, ignorant of the dependence of ideas on the relations of production, have assumed that the world was ruled by ideas.[349]

Marx finds that this concentration on thoughts, rather than on the material realities that determine thoughts, vitiates Stirner's whole conception of history. The description of the development of the individual from child to man deals with this development of his consciousness alone, ignoring the physical and social determinants of that consciousness.[350] The same lack of attention to social and material reality is evidenced in Stirner's account of world history, which is, indeed, merely a projection of his individual history onto a world scale:

> The entire unique history revolves around three stage: child, youth and man, who return "in various transformations" and in ever-widening circles until, finally, the entire history of the world of things and the world of spirit is reduced to "child, youth and man"....
>
> We spoke above of the German philosophical conception of history. Here, in Saint Max, we find a brilliant example of it. The speculative idea, the abstract conception, is made the driving force of history, and history is thereby turned into the mere history of philosophy. But even the latter is not conceived as, according to existing sources, it
>
> actually came about—not to mention how it developed under the influence of real historical relations—but as it was conceived and described by recent German philosophers, in particular Hegel and Feuerbach. And from these descriptions again only that was selected which could be adapted to the given end, and which came into the hands of our saint by tradition. Thus, history becomes a mere history of pseudo-ideas, a history about

349 *Ibid.*, p. 171.
350 *Ibid.*, p. 135.

spirits and specters, while the real, empirical history that forms the basis of this ghostly history is only utilized to provide bodies for these specters; from it are borrowed the names required to clothe these specters with the appearance of reality.[351]

Marx goes into a great deal of detail on Stirner's inadequate knowledge of the history of philosophy; these criticisms cannot be discussed here. It would be a subject for an independent investigation just how many of Marx's own historical points would still be considered valid today; even in regard to his own specialty, economic history, Engels admitted later that a re-reading of the chapter on Feuerbach "proved only how incomplete our knowledge of economic history still was at that time."[352] The important point here is not these details, but the purpose of Stirner's account of the history of the individual and the world, and whether he accomplished that purpose.

One of the results of this "religious" concentration on ideas rather than on reality is that Stirner winds up in a subjectivist, almost solipsist position. He appears to think that he has merely to "criticize" away the idea of the state in order for it to cease to exist in reality.

> Because the Holy is something alien, everything alien is transformed into the Holy; and because everything Holy is a bond, a fetter, all bonds and all fetters are transformed into the Holy. By this means Saint Sancho has already achieved the result that everything alien becomes for him a mere *appearance*, a mere idea, from which he frees himself by simply protesting against it and declaring that he does not have this idea.
>
> Just as we saw in the case of the egoist not in agreement with himself: people have only to change their

351 *Ibid.*, pp. 136-137.
352 Marx and Engels, *Selected Works*, II, 325.

consciousness to make everything in the world all right.[353]

The refusal to believe in this ideas of state, patriotism, loyalty, and so forth, is the basis of Stirner's concept of insurrection(*Empörung*—translated here as "rebellion"). And it is just because insurrection deals with ideas, and not with the actually existing social and economic conditions, that it is "impotent": "the difference between revolution and Stirner's rebellion is not, as Stirner thinks, that the one is a political and social act while the other is an egoistical act, but that the former is an act while the latter is no act at all."[354] True liberation can only be achieved through revolution, which is a social, not an individual act; no individual can free himself unless the rest of his society is also freed.[355] It turns out, therefore, that Stirner's "fantasy" liberation is in fact reactionary; it attempt to prevent real, effective revolution by offering consolation to the individual imprisoned in the *status quo*: "With him 'uniqueness' is nothing more than an embellishment of existing conditions, a little drop of comforting balm for the poor, impotent soul that has become wretched through wretchedness."[356]

Perhaps the most devastating criticism Marx directs at Stirner's "religious" thinking is that his central theme, the "ego" or *Einzige*, is itself nothing more than an empty abstraction. Stirner had prided himself on exposing the universals and ideals of others as mere abstractions, divorced from the true reality of the individual, corporeal human being; Marx turns the tables on him and asserts that the true reality is the social, with the individual consciousness having no independent existence. The so-called "individual" is nothing but a combination of social relationships: class, position in the division of labor, friendships, etc. If these are removed, what is left is not the bare "ego," but

353 Marx and Engels, *The German Ideology*, p. 311.
354 *Ibid.*, p. 423.
355 *Ibid.*, pp. 490-491.
356 *Ibid.*, p. 496.

nothing at all. The consciousness of the individual is a moment in the social whole, and can be abstracted from it only in thought. This is what Stirner has done; thus *"der Einzige"* is one more religious abstraction, along with "God," "Man," "Morality," and so forth.

> Hence it certainly follows that the development of an individual is determined by the development of all the others with whom he is directly or indirectly associated, and that the different generations of individuals entering into relation with one another are connected with one another, that the physical existence of the later generations is determined by that of their predecessors, and that these later generations inherit the productive forces and forms of association accumulated by their predecessors, their own mutual relations being determined thereby. In short, it is clear that a development occurs and that the history of a single individual cannot possibly be separated from the history of preceding or contemporary individuals, but is determined by this history.[357]

This "ego," according to Marx, has not been empirically discovered in the world—indeed, it could not be, since it does not exist—but has been constructed by Stirner out of still other categories by means of a Hegelian dialectic:

> "And so it is said": what was previously "One"...has become the "Ego"—the negative unity of realism and idealism, of the world of things and the world of spirit. Schelling calls this unity of realism and idealism "indifference" or, rendered in the Berlin dialect,[358] *"Jleichjiltigkeit"*; in Hegel it becomes the negative unity

---

357 *Ibid.*, p. 494.
358 Marx considers Berlin the center of "ideology," due to the lasting influence of Hegel.

in which the two moments are transcended. Saint Max who, like a real German speculative philosopher, is still tormented by this unity to be visible to him in the form of "corporeal individual", in a "fine fellow".... This "Ego" of Stirner's which is the final outcome of the hitherto existing world is, therefore, not a "corporeal individual", but a category constructed on the Hegelian method...[359]

Marx further accuses Stirner, who has nothing but thought-forms of categories to offer, of having only three of these: realism, idealism, and their *Aufhebung*, the Ego. Thus Stirner reveals poverty even in his stock-in-trade, ideas. It is the repeated dialectic of these three categories, disguised under different names, which for Marx constitutes the whole of *The Ego and His Own*.[360]

Furthermore, once again like the religious thinkers Stirner criticizes, Marx finds him preaching an ethics based upon his abstract idea. Feuerbach said that all men are essentially "Man"; similarly, Stirner finds that all men are essentially egoists, though unconscious or "involuntary" ones, and exhorts them to become in fact what they are in essence.[361] This moralistic attitude is especially unbecoming for Stirner; in fact, it is doubly inconsistent. Not only does he reject morality and then proceed to make moral demands, but the demands he makes are inconsistent with themselves. He is demanding of everyone that he become *unique*, different from all others, but it turns out that this "uniqueness" has a content, namely, the personality and attitudes of Stirner himself. In exhorting men to become unique, he is at the same time exhorting them to become all alike; the universal ideal is that everyone become a Stirner:

> Consequently, Saint Sancho could at most have said: for me, Saint Sancho, the State, religion, etc., are the Alien,

---

359 Marx and Engels, *The German Ideology*, pp. 208-209.
360 *Ibid.*, p. 136.
361 *Ibid.*, pp. 275-276.

the Holy. Instead of this he has to make them the absolutely Holy, the Holy for all individuals—how else could he have written his whole "Book"? How little it occurs to him to make each "Unique" the measure of his own "uniqueness"; how much he uses his own "uniqueness" as a measure, as a moral norm, to be applied to all other individuals, like a true moralist forcing them into his Procrustean bed, is already evident, *inter alia*, from his judgement on the departed and forgotten Klopstock. He opposes Klopstock with the moral maxim: he ought to have adopted an "attitude to religion altogether *his own*", and he would then arrive not at a *religion of his own*, which would be the correct conclusion..., but at a "dissolution and swallowing up of religion"..., a universal instead of a personal, unique result...Klopstock's attitude to religion is supposed to be not his "own", although it was altogether peculiar to him, and indeed was a relation to religion which made Klopstock Klopstock. His attitude to religion would have been his "own" only if he had behaved towards it not like Klopstock but like a modern German philosopher.[362]

As might be expected, Marx criticizes Stirner a great deal for his political theories. We will not go into Marx's lengthy attack on Stirner's "Union of Egoists," because it seems to result from taking Stirner's scattered hints and guesses as to what such an organization might look like, and deriving from them a full program that Stirner never intended.[363] We will, however, consider briefly Marx's reply to Stirner's criticism of communism ("social liberalism").

This section of "Saint Max" is, as one would again expect, rather long; a communist himself, Marx is especially concerned to refute Stirner's critique of communism. Marx's basic point

362 *Ibid.*, pp. 214-215.
363 *Ibid.*, pp. 453-468.

here is that "Saint Max" does not know what he is talking about, that he is arguing from a position of ignorance. Stirner is criticizing a communism which exists only in his imagination, having derived all his "factual information" third-hand from a government report hostile to communism.[364] In the first place, according to Marx, Stirner is mistaken in thinking that the communists desire to subordinate the individual to an imaginary collectivity called "society"; on the contrary, they wish to eliminate the present society. This is the only true way to liberate the individual, who is merely a part of the social organism, as the whole changes, so does the "individual":

> Saint Max believes that the communists wanted to "make sacrifices" to "society", when they want at most to sacrifice existing society; in this case he should have described their consciousness that their struggle is the common cause of all people who have outgrown the bourgeois system as a sacrifice that they make themselves.[365]

In the second place, Stirner falsely imputes to communism a concern with the "essence" of man, which turns out to be "man as worker." He thus seeks to depict communism as another variety of "religious thinking." But he is just seeing communism through his own religious spectacles; it cares nothing for "essences," but is directly involved with reality:

> With "Stirner", "communism" begins with searchings for "essence"; he wants again, like the good "youth", only to "penetrate behind things". That communism is a highly practical movement, pursuing practical aims by practical means, and that only perhaps in Germany, in opposing the German philosophers, can it spare a moment for the

---

364 I.e., the Bluntschli Report. Marx and Engels, *The German Ideology*, p. 229.
365 *Ibid.*, p. 233.

problem of "essence"—this, of course, is of no concern to our saint.[366]

Marx goes on to recommend that Stirner fill the void in his education concerning communism by consulting the writings of "the representative of English communism," Robert Owen, and defies him to find there "a passage containing anything of these propositions about 'essence', universal participation in labour, etc."[367]

Finally, we come to Marx's fundamental criticism of Stirner, which provides the explanation for all of the latter's other mistakes. Stirner's philosophy, it turns out, is fully accounted for by the fact that it is merely the ideology of the petty-bourgeois class. These small shopkeepers, independent peasants, civil servants, and members of the professions (Stirner himself was a "school-master," as Marx keeps reminding us) are perfect examples of Hegel's "civil society," the sphere of the *bellum omnium contra omnes*, of individualism, egoism, and self-seeking. It is only natural, then, that Stirner should develop a philosophy of egoism. Further, these petty bourgeois are in a very insecure position, hovering between the "big" bourgeoisie, whom they would like to join, and the proletariat, among whom they are afraid they may wind up after being ruined by competition from the big bourgeoisie. The proletariat, of course, is defined as a class by its lack of property; thus the primary concern of the petty bourgeois is to retain, and if possible to increase, his property. It is unavoidable, therefore, that Stirner should be so concerned about property that it appears in the title of his book (*Eigenthum*). Stirner is, then, the perfect ideological representative of the middle class, for whom Marx has nothing but contempt; of all classes, they have the least class-consciousness, and are continually wavering, siding now with the big bourgeoisie, now with the proletariat, concerned to protect their interests, but uncertain where their

---

366 *Ibid.*, p. 235.
367 *Ibid.*, pp. 235-236.

true interests lie.[368] Here, too, Stirner is completely in harmony with his class: he expresses this class-consciousness without even being aware of it:

> His sole service—rendered against his will and without his knowledge—was that he expressed the aspiration of the German petty bourgeois of today whose aim it is to become bourgeois. It was quite natural that the pettiness, timidity and constraint of the practical actions of these burghers should have as their counterpart the noisy, swaggering and impertinent boasting for all the world to hear of the "Unique" among their philosophical representatives. It is quite in accordance with the situation of the burghers that they do not want to know about their theoretical loudmouthed champion, while he knows nothing about them; that they are not in harmony with one another, and he is forced to preach egoism in agreement with itself. Now, perhaps, Sancho will realize the sort of umbilical cord that connect *his* ["Union"] with the Customs Union.[369]

5. Criticisms of Stirner: Modern Marxist Criticism

A 1966 book, *Die Ideologie der anonymen Gesellschaft* (*The Ideology of the Anonymous Society*), by Hans G. Helms, is a prodigious piece of work on Stirner, too long and complex to be examined in detail here, but too significant to be ignored. Helms

---

368 Bober, *Marx's Interpretation of History*, p. 105.
369 Marx and Engels, *The German Ideology*, p. 462. I have substituted "Union" for the translator's "Association"; the word in German is *Verein*. Cf. Marx and Engels, *Werke*, III, 396. The reference is to what we have been calling the "Union of Egoists." The substitution also makes Marx's pun come through in English: "Union"=*Verein*, "Customs Union"=*Zollverein*.

spends 503 pages analyzing Stirner's philosophy and document-ing the history of its influence from its first appearance to the present (at the end there is a 95-page bibliography listing all edi-tions and translations of Stirner's works and what would appear to be virtually all secondary sources up to 1966.)

In this section, only the main thrust of Helm's critique of Stirner can be presented, without even beginning to enter into the formidable array of historical details with which he buttress-es his argument. In the next chapter, the response to Helms will have to be conducted on the same general level.

Helms attacks Stirner from the modern Marxist point of view. His criticism is essentially Marx's in The German Ideology, brought up to date; Professor James J. Martin, perhaps the lead-ing American authority on Stirner, says that "in many ways he has just revived an old controversy which goes back to Stirner and Marx themselves."[370] What is new in Helm's treatment is that, in accordance with current Marxist theory, he sees fascism as one of the final stages of monopolistic capitalism, and the petty bour-geoisie as the source of support for fascist regimes; consequently, Stirner's philosophy, as the earliest important expression of the ideology of this class, is also a precursor of fascism and National Socialism. Helms states his thesis as follows:

> Fascism is the product of the middle class. Its ideology represents the false consciousness of the middle class, the class of administrators and distributors, the rest of the service occupations, the illusion-producers and the pro-ducers of the ideological illusion.
>
> The origin of fascism dates from the division of la-bor between the ownership of capital and the control of capital (control of production). The division took place as the Taylor system,[2371] and related systems of organi-

---

370 In a letter to the writer, May 14, 1971.
371 Helms evidently has in mind the work of Frederick W. Taylor, *The Principles of Scientific Management* (New York: Harper & Brothers,

zation and administration were introduced generally in the modern industrial states; though, indeed, in increasingly rarer instances the ownership of the means of production and control of production are still united in one hand.

These systems lead in the end to a development which was initiated much earlier through corporate property (shares): the gradual anonymization of property relations and administrative decrees. Through modern administrative mechanisms, the means of production and forces of production were detached from the fate of the individual owner. The control of the means and forces of production is placed in anonymous administrative-corporative private of public laws, which will regulate them according to arbitrary action and accident.

The division of labor of ownership and capital left the middle class a growing proportion of authority to decree, without raising them to be responsible proprietors or partners. The middle class rules by means of administration, in the name of the class of owners, the bourgeoisie. Representative democracy is its adequate political form of organization. Its varieties range from the free multi-party system over the "formed society" to the monocracy of a leader supported by two million camp-followers.

In Germany it was already abruptly executed at the time of the 1933 takeover of power by the middle class, prepared by the Weimar Republic, through Hitler— on good terms with the bourgeoisie. In countries like Sweden, England, and the USA it is proceeding gradually and unnoticed. Today the middle class is, by proxy, the ruling class in all modern industrial states. Its system of rule is the anonymous, statistically-controlled order.[372]

1911), although he gives no reference to it in the book.
372 Helms, *Die Ideologie der anonymen Gesellschat*, pp. 1-2 (my translation).

Stirner, as Marx has already pointed out, was the "apostle" of the middle class, as Marx and Engels were the "advocates" of the proletariat. But whereas Marxism is a scientific, realistic analysis of the actual situation facing the proletariat, and therefore an effective plan for action, Stirner, "instead of a socially determined analysis of the situation of the middle class,...presented an egoistic ideology."[373] Stirner's "ideology" corresponded, not to the actual conditions, but to the middle class's illusions about itself; therefore, it was useless as a program for action.

The advent of the "Taylor System" (or managerial revolution, as Burnham called it),[374] however, brought the relations of production into accord with Stirner's ideology; at the same time, by giving the middle class sole authority in administration, the economic situation made this class strong enough to absorb and act upon the ideology preached by Stirner:

> Because Stirner was not capable of formulating the class consciousness of the middle class, the immediate effect of the *Einzige* was small. In the period before the revolutions of 1848, the middle class was still too weak to be able to operate according to a radical ideology. The *Einzige* first became interesting to the middle class when it felt strong enough to lay stress upon its particular interests by means of a radical ideology.
>
> This background must be kept in mind by the reader: *Stirner did not create the ideology of the middle class: the origin of the ideology is a consequence of the social circumstances. The EINZIGE is merely its first significant formulation, he had an effect on the middle class only when the development of the conditions of production, administration, and distribution had made the middle class*

---

373 *Ibid.*, p. 3.

374 James Burnham, *The Managerial Revolution* (1941; Bloomington: Indiana University Press, 1962.)

susceptible to this effect.[375]

The middle class, wherever it exists (and it only exists in the advanced capitalist countries), is today the bearer of fascism, according to Helms; and the clearest statement of the fascist program is *The Ego and His Own*. Therefore, "it is this ideology which becomes the thermometer for the ideological embers smoldering in the brains of the middle class," and "the history of Stirnerism is at the same time the history of fascism."[376]

Helms then proceeds, for the next 499 pages, to document this thesis, marshalling an amount of evidence too great even to be outlined here. The general form of the book is as follows: after a general introduction to the concept of "ideology," Helms turns to a historical account of the social and economic circumstances of Stirner's time which were responsible for his thought; then he devotes several chapters to an analysis of the thought itself. This analysis is basically along the same lines as that in *The German Ideology*, but is organized systematically rather than as a "running commentary." For example, whereas Marx had scattered his comments on Stirner's styles throughout "Saint Max," Helms devotes a separate thirty-five page section to this topic, including two pages on Stirner's use of the dash. He then returns to the historical account, beginning with the "Stirner-Renaissance" of the 1890's, and traces the influence of Stirner up to and including the Third Reich, which he calls the "*Reich der Einzigen*." Needless to say, the triumph of National Socialism is held to be a triumph of Stirnerism. Helms concludes with a warning that the Federal Republic of Germany is in danger of a repetition of 1933 due to the continuing "virulent" influence of Stirner: "Of the present there is little good to report; of the future, evil is to be expected—a continuation of the fascist ideology is to be anticipated."[377]

---

375 Helms, *Die Ideologie der anonymen Gesellschaft*, pp. 3-4.
376 *Ibid.*, p. 4.
377 *Ibid.*, p. 491.

Max Stirner Versus Karl Marx

Chapter IV

CONCLUSION

In the Stirner-Marx controversy, the victory has usually been conceded to Marx; as Herbert Read puts it, "Marx triumphed over Stirner as he triumphed over Feuerbach and Bakunin: he had the last word and it is still echoing in the political events of the present day."[378] It is true that Marxism is a force in the world today, whereas Stirnerism is not (at least not under that name—allowing Helms' thesis for the moment that fascism and Stirnerism are identical). This practical victory of Marxism is, however, due to many external circumstances apart from the truth or falsity of the two theories. But even on this level, it is generally assumed that Marx's criticisms of Stirner in *The German Ideology* were conclusive for the most part, if not on every point. The object of

---

378 Read, *The Tenth Muse*, p. 75. Read goes on the say, however, as already noted, that "after a sleep of a hundred years the giants whom Marx thought he had slain show signs of coming to life again,"(*ibid.*), and that Stirner's doctrine of involuntary egoism has been confirmed by psychoanalysis, so that on this point "Marx's criticism...would need drastic revision to be convincing today" (p.79).

this chapter is to reopen this issue by attempting to respond, on Stirner's behalf, to the charges raised by Marx and Helms.

Stirner himself never had the opportunity to reply to the criticisms: obviously, he was long dead before Helms was born. But even in the case of his contemporary, Marx, this opportunity was denied to him. Marx and Engels were unable to publish *The German Ideology* in their own or Stirner's lifetimes, and "abandoned the manuscript to the gnawing criticism of the mice,"[379] where it remained until published by the Institute of Marxism-Leninism of the Soviet Union in 1932.[380]

The procedure in this chapter will be to take up each of the criticisms raised in the preceding chapter and to construct a reply to it, using Stirner's own words whenever possible. The goal is not to refute Marxism in order to set Stirnerism up in its place, but the more modest one of showing that Stirner's philosophy is at least a viable and possible alternative to Marxism. After dealing with Marx's and Helms's criticisms in turn, a final section will attempt to sum up the import of this entire work.

1. A Proper Standpoint for Considering the Replies

A special difficulty arises in placing Marxist and non-Marxist points of view in opposition, which is that from the Marxist perspective, the opposing viewpoint must be false; thus no fair, impartial hearing is possible. This situation is not due to personal prejudice or narrow-mindedness on the part of the individual Marxist, but is inherent in the nature of Marxism itself. The basic precept of Marxism is that there is and can only be one correct view of reality, and that is the materialist; all others are "ideologies" produced by a certain location in the relations of production of a given epoch. Like psychoanalysis, Marxism is irrefutable;[381]

---

379 Marx and Engels, *Selected Works*, I, 330.
380 Marx and Engels, *The German Ideology*, Introduction, p. 18.
381 Karl R. Popper, *The Open Society and its Enemies*, Vol. II: *The High Tide*

rather than enter into dialogue with an opposing theory, in order to test the relative truth-values of the two, it immediately or eventually relegates the other theory to the level of ideology, and thereby has done away with it.

In the present case, if this chapter is to be read from the Marxist standpoint, it would be better not to bother reading it at all. The replies on behalf of Stirner will then be taken as so many examples of false class-consciousness, proving nothing more than the degree of illusion that can be produced by social and economic circumstances. The only fruitful way to read this chapter is to prescind for the moment from the Marxist standpoint, to "bracket" it in the Husserlian sense, in order to allow the responses to stand on their own merits. This is not the same as conceding victory to Stirner; it may be that he is indeed a mouthpiece for middle class illusions. But this judgement should only be made after considering the arguments, and on the basis of evidence, rather than before seeing the arguments at all. If the Stirner-responses are approached with the expectation of discovering there an example of ideology, then it is virtually certain that that is exactly what will be discovered.

The standpoint that should be assumed for the purpose of considering the rest of this chapter, then, is a neutral one, outside both Marxism and Stirnerism, so that the possibility of Stirnerism as an alternative to Marxism may receive a hearing. I have tried to pave the way for this in the foregoing chapters by indicating the many similarities between Marx and Stirner, hoping to show that they are points along a continuum rather than polar opposites with no possibility of communication between them.

2. Possible Motivations for the Attack on Stirner

One good reason for taking Stirner seriously is that Marx

---

of Prophecy: Hegel, Marx, and the Aftermath (5th ed., revised; London: Routledge and Kegan Paul, 1966), pp. 267, 332 n. 30.

obviously did so himself. There are two features of the "Saint Max" which strike one almost immediately: its length and its unremitting, sarcastic hostility. In regard to the former, it has already been noted that the section on Stirner is far and away the longest part of the book, constituting two-thirds of its entire length, as opposed to a few pages on Marx's former mentor, Feuerbach. This is particularly surprising given the fact that there is so much repetition in Stirner; Marx could have summarized his main points in much less space, but instead chose to undertake a commentary. And the violence of the attack is truly incredible. Sidney Hook claims that "Marx, as distinct from all other of Stirner's erstwhile friends, gauged the positive merit of Stirner's work as well as the negative,"[382] but he is wrong on both counts. We shall see in a moment that some of Stirner's other "erstwhile friends" did indeed appreciate his work; as for Marx, I can find absolutely no acknowledgement of "positive merit" in *The German Ideology* (Hook may have had some other document in mind; he gives no source for this remark). There is evidence that Marx profited from his reading of Stirner, as will be pointed out presently; but if he did, he did not admit it in "Saint Max." On the contrary, the vituperation, sarcasm, and direct insult (for example, "blockhead") heaped upon Stirner is totally unremitting.

Other writers have noted these facts, and drawn from them the conclusion that Marx found Stirner's work extremely significant. In regard to the length of the section on Stirner, which he puts at three-quarters of that of the book (itself "an immense work"), Read notes that "Marx was not given to wasting his time on trivialities."[383] Paterson says that, after reading "Saint Max,"

> ...one realizes that Marx and Engels have involuntarily paid Stirner an astonishing tribute. With painstaking thoroughness they have dissected and annotated the whole of *Der Einzige und sein Eigenthum*,... chapter by

---

382 Hook, *From Hegel to Marx*, p. 173.
383 Read, *The Tenth Muse*, pp. 74-75.

chapter and section by section... there is not an argument, not a concept, barely a phrase which has escaped their fascinated analysis. Stirner could scarcely have expected more flattering attention from more eminent critics.[384]

Carrol, noting the length but paying special attention to the tone, concludes that the work shows Marx and Engels to have been afraid of Stirner:

Its composition and style suggest that in 1845 they considered Stirner to be their most dangerous adversary. The relentless, often vicious, ridiculing of him in this book cannot be passed off as merely the product of Marx's choleric temperament. "Saint Max" is the work of a mind under stress. Karl Löwith, in summing up this period, wrote: "The only thing radical enough to b compared to Marx is the converse programme of Stirner..."[385]

It seems clear that Marx and Engels regarded Stirner's work as a threat. There are several respects in which this is so. For one thing, as Paterson speculates, it may have been partly a matter of person pride, due to their

...consciousness of *Der Einzige* as an already standing judgement on "the German ideology"—a judgment which on some counts they had no desire to reverse, but as a whole they had to invalidate if they were to establish their own judgment as the final and uniquely authoritative one.[386]

But more significant is the fact that they saw a real

---

384 Paterson, *The Nihilistic Egoist: Max Stirner*, p. 107. I have corrected an obvious typographical error which appeared in the original.
385 Carroll, *Max Stirner: The Ego and His Own*, p. 14.
386 Paterson, *The Nihilistic Egoist: Max Stirner*, p. 106.

possibility that Stirner's critique of communism would, if not effectively combatted, carry the day among German radicals. Several of Stirner's "erstwhile friends" in the Young Hegelian movement had found *The Ego and His Own* very persuasive on this, if not on all, points. Feuerbach, in spite of the treatment accorded him in Stirner's book, was praising him in a letter in late 1844 as "the most gifted and freest writer it has been given to me to know."[387] Arnold Ruge, Marx's former co-editor on the *Deutsch-Französische Jahrbücher*, regarded Stirner as "the theoretical liberator" of Germany from the domination of abstract generalities such as "Society," "Equality," and "Humanity," which the socialists, in common with other German philosophers, were guilty of propagating. An associate of the Bauers, Gustav Julius, wrote that Marx's brand of socialism was essentially a Feuerbachian humanism, and as such, as Stirner had shown, a religious alienation; he noted that the reaction of the socialists to egoism, like that of the Christians to atheism, was one of "religious horror." Bruno Bauer continued this assault with an article in which he maintained that German socialists such as Marx, Engels, and Hess were Feuerbachians, and that Marx and Engels' *The Holy Family* was a desperate last attempt to defend humanism "against the liberating criticism of pure self-consciousness."[388]

There is strong evidence, then, to suggest that Marx himself regarded Stirner's philosophy as a serious competitor for public acceptance to his own system, and was determined to nip such a possibility in the bud both by defending himself against Stirner's attack, and by annihilating Stirner by plowing under the ashes. In the end, of course, even without the publication of *The German Ideology*, Marxism triumphed; but Marx and Engels could not be sure of this outcome, and made every effort to get the work published.

There is still another possibility suggested by the length, thoroughness, and tone of the "Saint Max," namely, that these

---

387 Carroll, *Max Stirner: The Ego and His Own*, p. 15.
388 Paterson, *The Nihilistic Egoist: Max Stirner*, pp. 108-109.

are symptoms which reveal a crisis point in Marx's own thought. Marx states that after failing to have the work published, he and Engels left it to the mice "all the more willingly as we had achieved our main purpose—self-clarification."[389] Allowing for a possible element of rationalization, we have Marx saying that the work of which the attack on Stirner forms the largest part was undertaken primarily in order to clarify his own thinking. Stirner may, then, have been instrumental in provoking a change in Marx's thought; Paterson believes the vehemence of Marx's attack to be an indication of this: "It was never Marx's habit to acknowledge any intellectual debts he might owe to a contemporary, and where a debt was contracted he tended to attack the errors and shortcomings of his creditor with augmented virulence and obduracy."[390]

Whether one subscribes to the thesis of a continuity in Marx's thought or to that of a sharp break, there can be no doubt that *something* occurred between *the Economic and Philosophical Manuscripts* written in the late summer of 1844, and the *Theses on Feuerbach*, written in March of 1845.[391] The former is supposed to be the *locus classicus* of the "young" Marx at the height of his infatuation with the Feuerbachian humanism, while the latter is, according to Engels, "the first document in which is deposited the brilliant germ of the new world outlook"[392] (which was then worked out at length in *The German Ideology*). Even if one holds that Marx's thought underwent no fundamental revision at this time, it is clear that his terminology began to take on an economic and scientific, rather than a philosophic, cast. There was a change of some kind; the question is, what prompted it?

The traditional interpretation is that Marx made the transition from Feuerbachianism to Marxism by his own unaided

---

389 Marx and Engels, *Selected Works*, I, 330.
390 Paterson, *The Nihilistic Egoist: Max Stirner*, pp. 121-122.
391 Source for these dates is Easton and Guddat, *Writings of the Young Marx*, pp. 283 and 400.
392 Marx and Engels, *Selected Works*, II, 25.

efforts, with Feuerbach the last influence on him before the "germ" of historical materialism appeared in the *Theses*. As McLellan and Paterson both point out, this is a misconception started by Engels in *Ludwig Feuerbach and the End of Classical German Philosophy* in 1886, which came to be "generally accepted as the unquestionable authority"[393] on the genesis of historical materialism. Here Engels gives a brief account of some of the other Young Hegelians (Stirner is dealt with in one sentence, and there wrongly linked with Bakunin),[394] then goes on to treat Feuerbach afterwards,

> thus giving the impression that this was the chronological order. This is belied by the dates themselves: Feuerbach's last significant contribution to the Young Hegelian debate was "Grundsätze der Philosophie der Zukunft", published in July 1843, whereas *Der Einzige* appeared late 1844,[395]

in November, to be exact. The evidence, then, indicates that Stirner's critique of Feuerbach was at least highly influential in prompting Marx's break with Feuerbach, and causing him to abandon such philosophical abstractions as "Man" in favor of the economic and historical analysis which has become identified with "Marxism." Paterson finds evidence that Stirner may have also been influential in the development of Marx's crucial concept of "praxis," the active, creative relation between man and his environment. He points out that the concept is "virtually absent from *The Holy Family* but...assumes increasing importance from the *Theses* on Feuerbach onwards." He refers to the first Thesis, which reads:

> The chief defect of all hitherto existing materialism—that

---

393 Paterson, *The Nihilistic Egoist: Max Stirner*, p. 104.
394 Marx and Engels, *Selected Works*, II, 332.
395 McLellan, *The Young Hegelians and Karl Marx*, p. 134.

of Feuerbach included—is that the thing, reality, sensuousness, is conceived only in the form of the *object*..or of *contemplation*..., but not *as human sensuous activity*, *practice*, not subjectively. Hence it appeared that the active side, in contradistinction to materialism, was developed by idealism—but only abstractly, since, of course, idealism does not know real, sensuous activity as such.[396]

Paterson goes on to ask:

Whose "idealism" is Marx referring to? Conventionally, he is assumed to be referring to classical Hegelianism in general, but this answer fails to explain why, at exactly *this* point in his development in the spring of 1845, Marx should suddenly have been brought to perceive the inherent "defect" of Feuerbachian materialism and to grasp the creative, revolutionary aspect of "idealism". One possibility, is that his punctual revolution from the dogmatic inertia of "all previous materialism" was due to his cathartic encounter with Stirner. Fresh from his study *of Der Einzige*, impressed against his will by its author's critical destruction of the immobile abstractions of orthodox metaphysics, Marx was free

to reject Stirner's subjectivism while absorbing and assessing the creative power of his dialectic. And at the beginning of 1845, if the philosophy of Feuerbach represented the highest expression of mechanistic materialism, the work of Stirner had notoriously carried the philosophy of dynamic "idealism" to its most extreme point of development.[397]

Paterson proceeds to list three more possible effects of Stirner on the evolution of Marx's thought. First, "Stirner's exposure of

396 Marx and Engels, *Selected Works*, II, 365.
397 Paterson, *The Nihilistic Egoist: Max Stirner*, pp. 119-120.

the endemic tendency of philosophical ideas, all of which are ultimately dependent for their existence on the concrete living thinker in whose mind they originate, to pose as autonomous realities with a life history of their own" is "vividly echoed in Marx's repeated criticisms of the philosophical 'reification' of ideas." Second, Stirner's "demonstration that so-called moral 'rights', including the 'natural right' to property, are meaningless unless supported by active material *power*, which indeed renders them otiose" is echoed in Marx's "rejection of the bourgeois notion of property rights; in his conviction that it is always social power, and never abstract principle, by means of which social conflicts are ultimately resolved." Third, Stirner's "attack on the negative liberal concept of 'freedom', which only amounts to 'freedom *from*' some restrictions, and his insistence that 'freedom to' enjoy the goods one covets (which is identical with power) must be forcibly *taken*" finds its echo "in Marx's rejection of the empty bourgeois concept of abstract 'freedom' in favor of the concrete freedom to create and enjoy the goods of society, as the sphere which a communist society will seek to enlarge."[398] Thus Paterson traces some of the most characteristic features of Marx's mature philosophy to their possible origins in Stirner.

In summary, then, there are strong indications that Marx's devastating attack on Stirner was prompted largely by the recognition that Stirner's philosophy was a very viable and real alternative to his own, both for others *and even for himself*. If this is the case, then the ridiculing, mocking, and insulting tone of "Saint Max" reveals, not the contempt that it indicates on the surface, but a profound respect. Marx himself, it would seem, saw Stirner as a formidable opponent, and brought out his heaviest weapons to defeat him. Whether that defeat did or did not take place, we will investigate in the following section.

---

398 *Ibid.*, p. 121.

Max Stirner Versus Karl Marx

3. Replies to Marx

Marx's general characterization of Stirner, as we saw in the last chapter, is that he is a "religious thinker," that is, one who is concerned only with thoughts and not with sensuous, concrete reality. It should be plain from the chapter on Stirner that he is at least not a "religious thinker" in the sense that he reifies universal concepts and worships them; it is against this that his whole polemic is directed. But the charge is still not true even if taken in the broader sense that for Stirner thoughts are the highest reality, and thinking is the supreme form of human activity. This was the position of the Bauers with their "critical criticism," but not that of Stirner, who makes it plain that he regards thought as one of his properties among others, and not to be given undue importance:

> I am no opponent of criticism. I am no dogmatist, and do not feel myself touched by the critic's tooth with which he tears the dogmatist to pieces. If I were a "dogmatist," I should place at the head of a dogma, a thought, an idea, a principle, and should complete this as a "systematist," spinning it out to a system, a structure of thought. Conversely, if I were a critic, an opponent of the dogmatist, I should carry on the fight of free thinking against the enthralling thought, I should defend the thinking against what was thought. But I am neither the champion of a thought nor the champion of thinking; for "I," from whom I start, am not a thought, nor do I consist in thinking. Against me, the unnamable, the realm of thought, thinking, and mind is shattered.[399]

A jerk does me the service of the most anxious thinking, a stretching of the limbs shakes off the torment of

---

399 Stirner, *The Ego and His Own*, pp. 147-148.

thoughts, a leap upward hurls from my breast the night-mare of the religious world, a jubilant Hoopla throws off year-long burdens.[400]

But finally, and in general, one must know how to "put everything out of his mind," I only to be able to—go to sleep.[401]

Stirner's deprecation of thought, in fact, leads him to an important, seemingly paradoxical insight into human psychology: that "creative thought" does not take place on the conscious level, but at some deeper, non-verbal level, from which it breaks through into consciousness. This is why Stirner refers to the Unique One as the "creative nothingness":

Language or "the word" tyrannizes hardest over us, because it brings up against us a whole army of *fixed ideas*. Just observe yourself in the act of reflection, right now, and you will find how you make progress only by becoming thoughtless and speechless every moment. You are not thoughtless and speechless merely in (say) sleep, but even in the deepest reflection; yes, precisely then most so. And only by this thoughtlessness, this unrecognized "freedom of thought" or freedom from the thought, are you your own. Only from it do you arrive at putting language to use as your property.[402]

Marx charges that Stirner's religious thinking is manifested in his accounts of individual and world history, which turn out to be nothing but intellectual histories with no attention paid to the economic substructure; he further contends that even this intellectual history is uninformed. The latter point must be

---

400 *Ibid.*, p. 148.
401 *Ibid.*, p. 334.
402 *Ibid.*, p. 346.

allowed to pass, as it would take us too far afield to go into it. But in regard to Stirner's lack of attention to empirical facts, one can point out that it was simply not part of his purpose to deal with those. He was concerned with a contemporary state of mind—as indeed Marx himself was in *The German Ideology*—and wanted to show the course of its development, prescinding for the moment from material considerations. Even Marx would admit the possibility, if not the usefulness, of such an account; in fact, he gives similar accounts himself, whenever, as in the Preface to *A Contribution to the Critique of Political Economy*, he gives his own intellectual autobiography. Here he describes the development of his thought as if it occurred simply as a result of the contact and interaction of his own opinions with those of others; there is no attempt to bring in economic considerations as causative factors, except for the fact that the "necessity of earning my living" by writing for the *New York Daily Tribune* forced him to keep abreast of current events to a greater extent than probably would have been the case otherwise.[403] Engels gives an even more extensive account in *Ludwig Feuerbach and the End of Classical German Philosophy*.[404] Marx and Engels are, therefore, subject to their own criticism. Stirner never denied that non-mental factors play a role in determining thinking, but it was not germane to his purpose to discuss their influence.

Stirner's position on the importance of thought seems rather to be this: that human behavior, whatever its ultimate causes, is in the final analysis the result of the conceptions, images, and beliefs that exist in the mind. This seems to be the import of the following statement about the influence of sensation:

> The sensuous is only that which exists for *the senses*; what, on the other hand, is enjoyable only to those who enjoy with *more* than the senses, who go beyond sense-enjoyment or sense-reception, is at most mediated or

---

403 Marx and Engels, *Selected Works*, I, 327-331
404 *Ibid.*, II, 324-364.

introduced by the senses, that is, the senses constitute a *condition* for obtaining it, but it is no longer anything sensuous. The sensuous, whatever it may be, when taken up into me becomes something non-sensuous, which, however, may again have sensuous effects, as by the stirring of my emotions and my blood.[405]

Marx would not disagree with this contention that the effects of the environment are mediated through the mind; he does not hold that human beings are unconscious automata which respond blindly to external conditions. On the contrary, their actions are always prompted by ideas, either false ideas—ideology—or true ones—historical materialism. The difference seems to be that for Marx, thought cannot change thought directly, but must do so through the medium of a change in the social conditions, by *praxis*. Stirner can be seen as attempting an experiment to determine whether criticism of certain ways of thinking can, without intervention of material conditions (other than speaking, hearing, writing and reading of books, etc.), change those ways of thinking, and, through them, human behavior.

The issue of revolution versus insurrection is apposite here. Marx said that Stirner's "insurrection" is not an act at all, because it has no practical effects; it is merely a change in attitude. But such a change in attitude can have practical consequences. Imagine an individual who, after reading Stirner's attacks on the state, patriotism, loyalty, and so on, decided to evade the draft, set up a clandestine printing press, and become a smuggler. These are unquestionably practical consequences.

Even so, Marx would contend that such individual insurrection is not an act in *his* sense, because it produces no general change in the *status quo*. Hence it is essentially reactionary, as opposed to revolution, which is a broad social movement resulting in widespread alteration of conditions. There are two replies to

---

405 Stirner, *The Ego and His Own*, p. 340.

this contention.

First, it is at least conceivable that Stirner's book could fall into large numbers of hands, and cause masses of people to lose their patriotic sentiments. If this phenomenon becomes widespread enough, the government of the country concerned could not stand without resorting to naked force; if the loss of patriotism spread to the soldiers and police; it would no longer be possible even to apply force. We have already quoted Stirner: "... can you imagine a State whose citizens one and all think nothing of it?" Marx sneers at this idea as utopian in "Saint Max"; nevertheless, he and Engels were trying to do essentially the same thing with their writings. They opposed terrorism and conspiracy, holding that the proper way to bring about the revolution was to produce the proper class consciousness in the proletariat. They seemed to feel that the latter effect would occur of itself eventually, as the proletariat's lot under capitalism became more degenerate; but they obviously also believed that they could hasten the process with their propaganda.[406] In other words, they, like Stirner, were endeavoring to transform thoughts directly by means of other thoughts. If their historical materialism is correct, this should have been an easy task for them, as the social conditions were ripe for revolution; their writings should have been enough to spark the conflagration. Their letters over many years are full of expectations that the revolution is about to occur; when it did occur, after their deaths, it was in a country where they had not expected it (although Marx had admitted

---

406 Bober (*Marx's Interpretation of History*, pp. 334-335) notes an inconsistency here: "In the development of human nature Marx places much emphasis on the effectiveness of the environment. What environment he foresees for the proletariat with the advance of capitalism is well known. The proletariat is plagues by the industrial reserve army, by increasing misery, and by the ravages of ever-deepening depressions. It is difficult to see how the masses so circumstanced can form a militant, intelligent unit. In the eyes of an environmentalist, especially, a race of degraded wage slaves is not a race of world builders."

that it could occur there)[407] by means of a small, conspiratorial party, directly influenced by their *ideas*, and not through a broad uprising of the proletariat, determined by economic conditions. Furthermore, the writings of Marx and Engels have appealed, not to the working class whose true consciousness they were supposed to reflect, but to the intelligentsia of the middle class, who should, on Marxist principles, be Stirnerians.

Second, even if it is true that Stirner's book does not provide a valid theory of social action, this is not a telling criticism of it. Stirner was primarily interested in the individual, not the society, which for him was at best just a collection of individuals and at worst an imaginary "fixed idea." His concern is with the integration of one's personality even under conditions one did not create; he shows how one can take action, here and now, to improve one's lot. Seen in this light, it is Marx whose theory is quietistic, and leads to no act at all. Marx holds that the individual is utterly powerless to change conditions on his own; he will be alienated, dehumanized, and exploited until the revolution, no matter what he may do. He can take action to promote the revolution, but he is ultimately dependent on others' following suit; if they do not, there is nothing for it but to keep trying and wait. If the revolution, like the Second Coming, turns out to be delayed beyond the lifetime of the present generation, then Marx offers the consolation—the "comforting balm for the poor, important soul," as he says against Stirner—that our children, or their children, will yet see a better world. It turns out, then, to be Stirner who provides the real *praxis*; Marx offers only hope.

We proceed to Marx's charge that Stirner's "Ego" is an abstract concept. Stirner's own statement that the Unique One, like God, is unnamable, has already been quoted in the chapter dealing with Stirner; it is only one of many such throughout the book. The import of all of them is that the Unique One is not a name for a concept at all, but the name of an entity which

---

407 Feuer, *Marx and Engels: Writings*, p. 439.

transcends all the conceptualization; it is a reality which cannot be fully grasped in thought. Marx was not the only one who missed this point; Feuerbach also advanced against Stirner that his "egoist" is merely another predicate, but a meaningless one. We quote here in part Stirner's reply to Feuerbach:

> The unique one is a statement, which, it is conceded with all openness and honesty—states nothing. Man, spirit, true individual, personality, etc., are statements or predicates which abound in a fullness of content, phrases of the highest matter. The unique one is, in contrast to those holy and sublime phrases, the empty, unpretentious, and thoroughly common phrase...
>
> Since the content of the unique one is not thought content, it is also unthinkable and unspeakable, and since it cannot be uttered, this perfect phrase is at the same time—*no phrase*.
>
> Only when *nothing* is stated about you and you are only named, are you acknowledged as yourself. As long as something is stated about you, you are only acknowledged as this something (man, mind, Christ, etc.). But the unique one states nothing, since he is only a name; he merely says that you are you and nothing other than you that you are a unique you, or you yourself. Hereby you are unpredicated, and at the same time without determination, vocation, law, etc.
>
> Speculation was adjusted to find a predicate which would be so *general* that it would comprehend each one. Such a predicate however should certainly not express what each *ought* to be, but rather what he *is*. Hence, if the predicate were "man", it must not be taken as what each *ought* to become, for otherwise all those who have not yet become this would be excluded, but rather as what each is. But this *what* is indeed an expression of *the universal* in each one, for *what* each has in common with

the other, but it is not an expression of the *each*, it does not express *who* each is. Are you exhaustively described when it is said that you are a man? Does one thereby also express *who* you are? Does every predicate "man" accomplish the task of the predicate, to express the subject *completely*, or does not it on the contrary omit the very subjectivity of the subject, not saying who, but merely what, the subject is?[408]

Marx further claims that this "concept" is arrived at by a Hegelian dialectical juggling with only three categories—realism, idealism, and negative unity of both—plus a few "auxiliary categories," whatever this may mean. It is true that Stirner uses a Hegelian method; so does Marx, and admits it, although he claims to have turned it right side up. The charge of a paucity of categories can be directed right back at Marx, who imposes his "relations of production" and "mode of production" upon virtually every subject he treats, along with a few "auxiliary categories" such as "praxis," "class," and so on.

Marx contends that Stirner has misconceived the individual as independent of his social relations, whereas man is in fact innately social and is constituted by those relations. But Stirner does recognize that man is originally social; he contends, however, that the consciousness of individuality can be achieved:

> Not isolation or being alone, but society, is man's original state. Our existence begins with the most intimate conjunction, as we are already living without mother before we breathe; when we see the light of the world, we at once lie on a human being's breast again, her love cradles us in the lap, leads us in the gocart, and chains us to her person with a thousand ties. Society is our *state of nature*. And this is why, the more we learn to feel ourselves, the

---

408 Mackay, *Max Stirners kleinere Schriften*, pp. 115-117; translated by Carroll, *Max Stirner: The Ego and His Own*, pp. 257-258.

Max Stirner Versus Karl Marx

connection that was formerly most intimate becomes ever looser and the dissolution of the original society more unmistakable. To have once again for herself the child that once lay under her heart, the mother must fetch it from the street and from the midst of its playmates. The child prefers the *intercourse* that is enters into with *its fellows* to the society that it has not entered into, but only been born in.[409]

Stirner understands that the individual does not create himself and his character *ex nihilo*, that many outside influences are at work on him. He does, however, deny that all of these influences are on the same level. The individual who has achieved consciousness of his individuality can select those influences which he wants to incorporate into his being, and rejects others:

> When one's own is contrasted with what is *imparted* to him, there is no use in objecting that we cannot have anything isolated, but receive everything as part of the universal order, and therefore through the impression of what is around us, and that consequently we have it as something "imparted"; for there is a great difference between the feelings and thoughts which are *aroused* in me by other things and those which are given to me....
>
> The difference is, then, whether feelings are imparted to me or are only aroused. Those which are aroused are my own, egoistic, because they are not *as feelings* drilled into me, dictated to me, and pressed upon me; but those which are imparted to me I receive, with open arms—I cherish them in me as a heritage, cultivate them, and am *possessed* by them.[410]

The mere fact that, historically, the concept of individuality

---

409 Stirner, *The Ego and His Own*, pp. 305-306.
410 *Ibid.*, pp. 65-66.

may have arisen late, and that the human being for eons felt himself as part of a larger whole (tribe, etc.), says nothing about the truth or falsity of the idea of individuality; it says only that it is late. On the same basis, one could argue that black magic was superior to modern medicine, because the latter was only a late development. Once the feeling of individuality arises, it is simply there, and must be recognized. Nor does the fact that no one human could survive for long, or accomplish anything, mean that he is somehow indissolubly linked to every other human being in the world, past, present, and future. At the most it means that he is linked to those who have actually assisted him in some way, and has no connection whatever to the rest. For Stirner, all such arguments are merely rationalizations for the persistence of the "fixed ideas" of humanity, society, and so forth, calculated to persuade us to feel that we "owe" something to these ideas:

> The beautiful dream of a "social duty" still continues to be dreamed. People think again that society *gives* what we need, and we are *under obligations* to it on that account, owe it everything. They are still at the point of wanting to *serve* a "supreme giver of all good." That society is no ego at all, which could give, bestow, or grant, but an instrument or means, from which we may derive benefit; that we have no social duties, but solely interests for the pursuance of which society must serve us; that we owe society no sacrifice, but, if we sacrifice anything, sacrifice it to ourselves—of this the Socialists do not think, because they—as liberals—are imprisoned in the religious principle, and zealously aspire after—a sacred society, such as the State was hitherto.[411]

Marx's final accusation against Stirner under the heading of "religious thinking" is that Stirner espouses an ethics. The reply

---

411 *Ibid.*, p. 123.

to this is simply a flat denial. The Ego and His Own is totally consistent in that it is the expression of a particular self, Stirner's self. He does not exhort his readers to become egoists; at most, by means of many examples, he tries to reveal to them that they are already egoists, but egoists operating in a self-defeating manner. He does not argue that the ideas of patriotism, morality, piety, and so on are illusions, and that *therefore* one *ought* to live one's life in a different manner; rather, he attempts to reveal these ideas as illusions, and offers himself as an example of a life free from illusions. His book is really a form of psychotherapy; Stirner tries to expose to the reader the sources of his confusions and frustrations, and leaves it to the reader to take or not to take action to rid himself of these confusions. Contrary to Marx's assertion, Stirner sets up no "ideal" self to which he exhorts men to approximate; the whole thrust of his book is to combat such conceptions:

> If religion has set up the proposition that we are sinners altogether, I set over against it the other: we are perfect altogether! For we are, every moment, all that we can be; and we never need be more. Since no defect cleaves to us, sin has no meaning either. Show me a sinner in the world still, if no one any longer needs to do what suits a superior! If I only need do what suits myself, I am no sinner if I do not do what suits myself, as I do not injure in myself a "holy one"; if, on the other hand, I am to be pious, then I must do what suits God; if I am to act humanly, I must do what suits the essence of man, the idea of mankind, etc....
>
> We are perfect altogether, and on the whole earth there is not one man who is a sinner! There are crazy people who imagine that they are God the Father, God the Son, or the man in the moon, and so too the world swarms with fools who seem to themselves to be sinners; but, as the former are not the man in the moon, so the

latter are—not sinners. Their sin is imaginary.

Yet, it is insidiously objected, their craziness or their possessedness is at least their sin. Their possessedness is nothing but what they—could achieve, the result of their development, just as Luther's faith in the bible was all that he was—competent to make out.[412]

The psychotherapeutic nature of Stirner's project becomes apparent here. Those who are "possessed" by religion, morality, humanitarianism, and so forth, are considered literally to be mentally ill by Stirner. Their mental illness consists in the fact that they do not view reality as it is, but through the medium of various distorted thoughts. This perception has an effect on their practice, as it does in the case of any psychosis; in this case, it reveals itself in, among other things, *autos-da-fé*, wars, reigns of terror, purge trials, and untold human misery. It is true that Stirner, like any psychiatrist, considers sanity a more desirable condition than insanity; if this constitutes an ethics, so be it, but it is a very broad conception of ethics.

Marx contends that Stirner's attack on communism is misguided, in that the communists do not, in the first place, wish to subordinate the individual to the society. This is a very complicated point, hinging largely on definitions of terms. Marx, of course, claims that communists want to "free" the individual; but at the same time, his conception of individuality is social in nature. He is confident that when communism has been fully realized, there will be no conflict between individual and social interests; in order for this to be the case, however, a high degree of homogeneity must be presumed among the individuals constituting the society. Marx recognizes that such homogeneity does not prevail at present owing to the division of labor; nor does he expect it to arise automatically after the revolution. This is why he allows for the intermediate stage of the dictatorship of the proletariat,

---

412 *Ibid.*, 359.

during which the working class will exercise government power to abolish private property and eliminate class distinctions. To Marx, this leveling of everyone to a common denominator is liberation; to Stirner, it is the sacrificing of individuality to society.

Marx also charges that Stirner is wrong in thinking that the communists are concerned with human essence. We have already quoted, in the preceding chapter, passages from Marx's younger writings which show clearly that he, like the communists depicted by Stirner, conceived labor as the essence of "species-being" of man. It is true that in his later writings such talk is dropped in favor of historical and economic analysis; nevertheless, it is clear that nothing has substantially changed. It is still the proletarian—the laborer—who is the focus of Marx's attention; it is still he who will liberate society and establish the new order in which class strife will be at an end. The only difference is that this prediction is now supposed to result from empirical observation rather than philosophical speculation; one must assume that it is merely a happy coincidence that the two happen to coincide so perfectly. And, regardless of whether the difference between the young and the mature Marx is one of the doctrine or merely one of terminology, it is likely, as has already been pointed out, that the change was at least partially a result of Marx's encounter with Stirner. McLellan states that

> ...it is worth while noting...that the writings referred to as a refutation of Stirner's attack on "essence"...are not those of Marx or Hess, but those of Owen. Though it is certainly true that the ideas in the *Deutsche Ideologie* are different from those criticized by Stirner, it is reasonable to suppose that these differences are, to a considerable extent, due precisely to that criticism.[413]

Finally, Marx's fundamental criticism of Stirner is that the

---

413 McLellan, *The Young Hegelians and Karl Marx*, p. 134.

latter represents the ideology of the petty bourgeoisie. Such a criticism flies in the face of Stirner's reiterated mocking of everything the middle class holds dear. Stirner recognized the existence of "bourgeois morality," and also recognized its close connection with the economic concerns of the bourgeoisie:

> The [bourgeoisie] professes a morality which is most closely connected with its essence. The first demand of this morality is to the effect that one should carry on a solid business, an honorable trade, lead a moral life. Immoral, to it, is the sharper, the demirep, the thief, robber, and murderer, the gamester, the penniless man without a situation, the frivolous man. The doughty burgher designates the feeling against these "immoral" people as his "deepest indignation."
>
> All these lack settlement, the *solid* quality of business, a solid, seemly life, a fixed income, etc.; in short, they belong, because their existence does not rest on a *secure basis*, to the dangerous "individuals or isolated persons," to the dangerous *proletariat*; they are "individual brawlers" who offer no "guarantee" and have "nothing to lose" and so nothing to risk. The forming of family ties *binds* a man: he who is bound furnishes security, can be taken hold of; not so the street-walker. The gamester stakes everything on the game, ruins himself and others—no guarantee. All who appear to the [bourgeois] suspicious, hostile, and dangerous might be comprised under the name "vagabonds"; every vagabondish way of living displeases him. For there are intellectual vagabonds too, to whom hereditary dwelling-place of their fathers seems too cramped and oppressive for them to be willing to satisfy themselves with the limited space any more: instead of keeping within the limits of a temperate style of thinking, and taking as inviolable truth what furnishes comfort and tranquility to thousands, they overleap all

bounds of the traditional and run wild with their impudent criticism and untamed mania for doubt, these extravagated vagabonds.[414]

It must be conceded to Marx that there are some superficial similarities between Stirner's position and middle-class ideals: his "egoism" does remind one of the stand of the self-reliant, independent small businessman or farmer, and he does not even use the expression "war of all against all," which Hegel uses to characterize civil society. But Stirner sees through the empty ideology of "free competition" as it exists in bourgeois society:

> There is a rich manufacturer doing a brilliant business, and I should like to compete with him. "Go ahead," says the State, "I have no objection to make to your *person* as competitor." Yes, I reply, but for that I need a space for buildings, I need money! "That's bad; but, if you have no money, you cannot compete. You must not take anything from anybody, for I protect property and grant it privileges." Free competition is not "free," because I lack the THINGS for competition. Against my *person* no objection can be made, but because I have not the things my person too must step to the rear. And who has the necessary things? Perhaps that manufacturer? Why, from him I could take them away! No, the State has them as property, the manufacturer only as fief, as possession.
>
> But, since it is no use trying it with the manufacturer, I will compete with that professor of jurisprudence; the man is a booby, and I, who know a hundred times more than he, shall make his classroom empty. "Have you studied and graduated, friend?" No, but what of that? I understand abundantly what is necessary for instruction in that department. "Sorry, but competition is not 'free'

414 *Ibid.*, 262.

here. Against your person there is nothing to be said, but the *thing*, the doctor's diploma, is lacking. And this diploma I, the State demand. Ask me for it respectfully first; then we will see what is to be done.[415]

It appears from this quotation, too, what Stirner thinks about the "sacred rights of property," so dear to the bourgeoisie. Marx contends that Stirner's preoccupation with property marks him unmistakably as a spokesman for the petty bourgeoisie; but Stirner uses the word(*Eigenthum*) to designate something quite different from material goods or land. Primarily, the individual's "property" signifies his personal characteristics or "properties"(*Eigenschaften*). The following passages should make this clear:

> The long and the short of it is this: that we are men is the slightest thing about us, and has significance only in so far as it is one of our *qualities*, our property. I am indeed among other things a man, as I am a living being, therefore an animal, or a European, a Berliner, and the like...[416]
> But my property is not a thing, since this has an existence independent of me; only my might is my own. Not this tree, but my might or control over it, is what is mine.[417]

Property is decidedly not the be-all and end-al for Stirner, as it is for the bourgeoisie; such an attitude Stirner regards as one more form of possession. The individual must raise himself above his property, make it a matter of relative indifference to himself. This applies to intellectual property, such a philosophical positions, as much as to material property:

Doubtless, as owner of thoughts, I shall cover my

---

415 *Ibid.*, pp. 174-175.
416 *Ibid.*, p. 276.
417 *Ibid.*, p. 358.

property with my shield, just as I do not, as owner of things, willingly let everybody help himself to them; but at the same time I shall look forward smilingly to the outcome of the battle, smilingly lay the shield on the corpses of my thoughts and my faith, smilingly triumph when I am beaten. That is the very humor of the thing. Everyone who has "sublime feelings" is able to vent his humor on the pettinesses of men; but to let it play with all "great thoughts, sublime feelings, noble inspiration, and sacred faith" presupposes that I am the owner of all.[418]

For Stirner, property and even life itself are not to be hoarded, but to be used up, "squandered." This is directly opposite to the bourgeois idealization of saving, accumulation, and the deferring of immediate for long-range satisfactions, as Marx himself-described them less than two years prior to the writing of *The German Ideology*:

Political economy, the science of *wealth*, is therefore at the same time, the science of renunciation, of privation and of saving, which actually succeeds in depriving man of fresh *air* and of physical *activity*. This science of a marvelous industry is at the same time the science of asceticism. Its true ideal is the *ascetic* but *usurious* miser and the *ascetic* but *productive* worker who takes a part of his wages to the savings bank...Thus, despite its worldly and pleasure-seeking appearance, it is a truly moral science, the most moral of all sciences. Its principal thesis is the renunciation of life and of human needs. The less you eat, drink, buy books, go to the theatre or to balls, or to the public house, and the less you think, love, theorize, sing, paint, fence, etc. the more will you be able to save and the *greater* will become your treasure which neither

---

418 *Ibid.*

moth nor rust will corrupt—your *capital.* The less you *are,* the less you express your life, the more you *have,* the greater is your *alienated* life and the greater is the savings of your alienated being.[419]

Opposed to this morality of self-denial and investment is the philosophy of wastefulness and enjoyment by Stirner:

> When one is anxious only to live, he easily, in this solicitude, forgets the enjoyment of life. If his only concern is for life, and he thinks "if I only have my dear life," he does not apply his full strength to using, that is, enjoying, life. But how does one use life? In using it up, like the candle, which one uses in burning it up. One uses life, and consequently himself the living one, in *consuming* it and himself. *Enjoyment of life* is using life up....
>
> Henceforth, the question runs, not how one can acquire life, but how he can squander, enjoy it; or, not how one is to produce the true self in himself, but how one is to dissolve himself, to live himself out.[420]

In order to support his charge that Stirner is a spokesman for the bourgeoisie, Marx is forced in *The German Ideology* to invent, *ad hoc,* a whole new historical account of the development of "the philosophy of enjoyment," tracing it to the decline of feudalism and maintaining that the bourgeoisie are its modern upholders.[421] He appears to forget this analysis again in *Capital,* in which he attributes the crises of underconsumption, which help to bring about the downfall of capitalism, partly to the tendency of the bourgeoisie to save and invest rather than to consume.[422]

---

419 Marx, *Economic and Philosophical Manuscripts,* in Fromm, *Marx's Concept of Man,* p. 144.

420 Stirner, *The Ego and His Own,* p. 320.

421 Marx and Engels, *The German Ideology,* pp. 470-471.

422 See *supra,* p. 116.

4. Replies to Helms

Once again, as in the preceding chapter, it is possible to deal only in the most cursory manner with the criticisms of Helms, due to the massive nature of his work. It is noteworthy that Helms's attack on Stirner surpasses in magnitude even that of Marx in *The German Ideology*, indication that at least one modern Marxist agrees with the founder of Marxism in recognizing Stirner as a formidable opponent. Once again, the thesis of the present work, that Stirner represents the most viable alternative to Marxism, appears to be recognized by the Marxists themselves.

Helms's basic contention is that Stirner is the ideological representative of the middle class, and that this ideology is expressed in practice in the form of fascist totalitarianism.

Taking the first part of this charge separately, we note that it is essentially the same as that advanced by Marx; we have already seen serious reasons to believe that it was mistaken. But Helms's renewal of the charge presents difficulties all its own, even from a strictly Marxist point of view. Helms claims, as noted previously, that the economic situation of the middle class has changed enormously since Stirner's time, due to the so-called "managerial revolution": the middle class no longer consists just of shopkeepers, school teachers, and small farmers, all of them impotent politically and fearful of becoming proletarianized. Rather, it is now the class of administrators, and so, "by proxy, the ruling class in all modern industrial states." It is this change in its position of power that has made the middle class for the first time "susceptible" to Stirner's work.

What is hard to understand here is how Stirner's work, or indeed any one work, could be the ideological expression both of the impotent middle class of 1844 and the omnipotent middle class of 1966. Ideology, according to the Marxists, is the distorted consciousness, produced by economic conditions, of a given class, and changes as the economic conditions change. Helms admits that the economic circumstances of the middle class have changed enormously since the mid-nineteenth century; how, then, could the ideology have stayed the same? In effect, Stirner in 1844 was giving voice to the consciousness of a class which did not actually come into existence until over fifty years later. This would make Stirner a much more accurate prophet than Marx, whose predictions of a world-wide proletarian revolution have yet to be realized; and this would indicate that Stirner's philosophy represents a more realistic insight into the actual conditions than does Marx's. Hence it must be Marx, not Stirner, who expresses an "ideology," and Stirner, not Marx, who possesses the "scientific" point of view. Helm's conclusion appears to be inconsistent with his historical-materialist premises.

Helms qualifies his thesis still further, and removes it still further from empirical reality, when he admits that not all, or even a majority, of the middle class knows of Stirner, and that Stirner holds as much appeal for members of other classes:

> There have been and are readers and followers of Stirner in all imaginable groups, large and small, even in the proletariat and in the bourgeoisie. This does not mean that everyone read Stirner or that the whole middle class had absolute confidence in him. It does mean that Stirner's ideology, in principle, could and can be accepted and adapted by the self-consciousness of the average member of the middle class. The interest of the "*Einzige*" conforms to the interest of the proverbial "man in the street." Therin rests Stirner's virulence and actuality.[423]

It is now difficult to know just what is being claimed. Stirner is supposed to express the ideology of the middle class, but not necessarily to have had much influence on the middle class; furthermore, it appears that he has had at least as much influence on other classes, whose consciousness he does *not* represent;

---

423 Helms, *Die Ideologie der anonymen Gesellschaft*, p. 4.

Stirner's philosophy could "in principle" be accepted and *adapted* by the "average" member of the middle class—whatever "in principle" means, whatever the "average" member is and however this is ascertained, and whatever degree of distortion would still be considered "adaptation"; finally, Stirner's "interest" happens to coincide with that of the "man in the street"—who could be a proletarian just as easily as a member of the middle class.

On the basis of this faulty analysis, in conjunction with the Leninist thesis that fascism is one of the last phases of capitalism, Helms goes on to characterize Stirner's philosophy as fascism. It is this thesis which the bulk of the book is given over to documenting. Helms himself, however, reveals the sort of "documentation" he has undertaken:

> The ideological situation in the Federal Republic of Germany is the occasion, its dangerous development the motor, of this work. Its content is the analysis and historical genesis of the currently reigning ideology; its sense is to work against its powers. The interlacing of analytic and political intentions forbids an illusory "neutral" presentation of the documents; the documents are, rather, used for the desired polemic against the ideology, its teachers, and its unwitting supporters. In the analysis of the ideology and its historical stages of development, no feigning of abstract considerations is permissible.[424]

In other words, instead of an empirical inquiry resting on evidence, we have what is admittedly an attempt to bend the evidence to support a conclusion arrived at *a priori* on theoretical grounds. The result has been described by John Carroll, who is himself somewhat sympathetic to the idea that Stirner may have some links to fascism, as a "savage misreading" of Stirner.[425] He says:

---

424 *Ibid.*, p. 1.
425 Carroll, *Max Stirner: The Ego and His Own*, p. 264.

Looking at the dichotomy between Stirner and Marx from the Marxist standpoint, as Helms does, Stirner becomes the first ideologist of the middle class and one of the precursors of fascism. However, he is blatantly misrepresented by this interpretation and its determination to search out the economic class to which some of his ideas seem most appropriate. It disregards the most important aspects of his work—his psychology, his analysis of morality, and his critique of Christianity and liberalism. Helms, in his Marxist attempt to place Stirner in the "roots of the right", had to strain possible associations to the extent of referring to "the existentialist wave of sublimated fascism".[426]

The associations are indeed strained, and Helms admits this, too. He refers to the "historically modified interpretation" and "the often extremely mediated influences of Stirner."[427] What this amounts to is, as a reviewer notes, that "Helms set up as witnesses several 'Stirnerites,' who had misunderstood Stirner in the same way as he himself had."[428] A few examples of Helm's "associations" may be noted. He produces two quotations from Mussolini's prison writings in which Stirner is mentioned. One of these, however, also mentions "Nietzsche, Goethe, Schiller, Montaigne, Cervantes, etc."[429] If this is evidence for Stirner's influence on fascism, it is equally evidence for the influence of all the others listed, including Cervantes, who was one of Marx's favorite authors.[430] Furthermore, as Carroll points out, "Mussolini's notorious exhibitionism made him less a passionate follower of ideas

426 Ibid., p. 15
427 Helms, *Die Ideologie der anonymen Gesellschaft*, p. 4.
428 Kurt Zube, Review of *Die Ideologie der anonymen Gesellschaft*, Erlesenes, No. 1 (1967-68), p. 62. Translation by Robert H. Beebe, unpublished.
429 Helms, *Die Ideologie der anonymen Gesellschaft*, p. 11.
430 Paul Lafargue, "Reminiscences of Marx," in Fromm, *Marx's Concept of Man*, p. 225. The section on Stirner in *The German Ideology* contains numerous quotations from and allusions to *Don Quixote*.

than an intellectual opportunist, freely swapping them to suit the cause of the moment."[431]

As for a direct influence of Stirner on Nazism, Helms can do no better than the following:

> The citing of analogous documents to Stirner from National Socialist literature was also foregone. These are widely dispersed, easily accessible and well enough known. There is no difficult in producing a catalog of parallel passages in the "*Einzige*" and in *Mein Kampf*. That does not mean that Hitler knew and got the full value out of the "*Einzige*," although according to the material quoted in the appendix to Chapter XII, a Stirner-influence on Hitler mediated through Dietrich Eckart is at least not to be excluded. It does mean that Hitler articulated a specific middle-class ideology and that Stirnerism and National Socialism are variations of the same fascist ideology.[432]

Helms also hints that he has merely scratched the surface in regard to the influences of Stirner on National Socialism: "Moreover, it should be kept in mind that the analyzed and bibliographically ascertained materials are by no means complete. They represent only a proportionately small part of what might actually exist."[433]

We have to take Helm's word for it that there *might* exist other materials showing Stirner's part in the rise of National Socialism; all he shows in the aforementioned appendix is that Eckart, who supported Hitler financially in the early 1920's, borrowed some ideas from Stirner. Carroll, however, points out that "it is clear that [Eckart] was far from an enthusiastic Stirnerian; he was much more profoundly influenced by the parallel individualism

---

431 Carroll, *Max Stirner: The Ego and His Own*, p. 13.
432 Helms, *Die Ideologie der anonymen Gesellschaft*, p. 5.
433 Ibid., p. 4.

of Ibsen's Peer Gynt."[434] Far more important intellectually to Nazism than Eckart was Alfred Rosenberg, "the Nazis' official 'philosopher,'"[435] author of *The Myth of the Twentieth Century*. Rosenberg's book, a best-seller in Germany in the 1930's, contains a laudatory chapter on Schopenhauer, and praises Plato as a philosopher of dictatorship but does not mention Stirner.[436] Nor is Rosenberg mentioned in Helms's book.

Helms does not, then, present very convincing evidence that leading figures in the National Socialist movement were influenced by Stirner, or that many of them, including Hitler himself, had even heard of him. But even had Helms established this, it would not be sufficient to show that Stirner was responsible for Nazism. Carroll asks:

> Are we to accept the view that theory contains within itself its own praxis, in the sense that the way it is used represents a part of its own inner reality? Is the manner in which an idea is interpreted, and that interpretation realized, essential to its ontological nature? Does the fact that Mussolini was enthusiastic about his work make Stirner in any way responsible for the atrocities of Italian fascism? There is clearly no simple answer...[437]

Stirner had an answer to this question, at least in regard to his own work (and this answer should also lay to rest the allegation that Stirner was actually a moralist):

> Do I write out of love to men? No, I write because I want to procure for *my* thoughts an existence in the world;

---

434 Carroll, *Max Stirner: The Ego and His Own*, p. 14.

435 Kaufmann, "The Hegel Myth and Its Method," in Kaufmann, *Hegel's Political Philosophy*, p. 147.

436 Alfred Rosenberg, *Der Mythus des 20. Jahrhunderts* (München: Hoheneichen-Verlag, 1939).

437 Carroll, *Max Stirner: The Ego and His Own*, p. 13.

and, even if I foresaw that these thoughts would deprive you of your rest and your peace, even if I foresaw the bloodiest wars and the fall of many generations springing up from this seed of thought—I would nevertheless scatter it. Do with it what you will and can, that is your affair and does not trouble me. You will perhaps have only trouble, combat, and death from it, very few will draw joy from it. If your weal lay at my heart, I should act as the church did in withholding the Bible from the laity, or Christian governments, which make it a sacred duty for themselves to "protect the common people from bad books."[438]

Moreover, Helms, who obviously wishes to reply in the affirmative to Carroll's question, is in a difficult position. Regardless of whether Stirner did or did not influence the fascists, it is indisputable that Marx influenced modern communism. By Helm's reasoning, then, the atrocities of the Stalinist era, the Berlin Wall, and the incarceration of dissidents in Soviet insane asylums must all be laid directly at Marx's door, however horrified Marx himself might have been had he foreseen such events.

It is very difficult to understand, when one looks at Stirner's actual words, how he could ever be associated with fascism: He repudiates virtually every fascist tenet. One of the characteristics of fascism is the totalitarian state; such a state can find little support in comments such as the following:

> States last only so long as there is a *ruling will* and this ruling will is looked upon as tantamount to the own will. The lord's will is—law. What do your laws amount to if no one obeys them? What your orders, if nobody lets himself be ordered? The State cannot forebear the claim to determine the individual's will, to speculate and count

---

438 Stirner, *The Ego and His Own*, p. 296.

on this. For the State it is indispensable that nobody have an *own will*; if one had, the State would have to exclude (lock up, banish etc.) this one; if all had, they would do away with the State. The State is not thinkable without lordship and servitude (subjection); for the State must will to be the lord of all that it embraces, and this will is called the "will of the State."[439]

How change it? Only by recognizing no *duty*, not binding myself nor letting myself be bound. If I have no duty, then I know no law either.

"But they will bind me!" My will nobody can bind, and my disinclination remains free.[440]

The importance of the party and of party loyalty is also typical of fascism; Stirner rejects parties, too:

In the State the *party* is current. "Party, party, who should not join one!" But the individual is *unique*, not a member of the party. He unites freely, and separates freely again. The party is nothing but a State in the State, and in this smaller bee-State "peace" is also to rule just as in the greater. The very people who cry loudest that there must be an *opposition* in the State inveigh against every discord in the party. A proof that they too want only a— State. All parties are shattered not against the State, but against the ego.[441]

Herbert Marcuse links the rise of fascism to the existentialist denial of the universal; this denial of universality is one of the leading similarities between Stirner and the existentialists. Here, then, might be a link between Stirner and fascism. Marcuse's argument runs as follows:

---

439 *Ibid.*, p. 195.
440 *Ibid.*, p. 196.
441 *Ibid.*, p. 235.

The concept of reason was connected with advanced ideas, like the essential equality of men, the rule of law, the standard of rationality in the state and society, and... Western rationalism was thus definitely linked with the fundamental institutions of liberalist society. In the ideological field, the struggle against this liberalism began with the attack on rationalism. The position called "existentialism" played an important part in this attack. First, it denied the dignity and reality of the universal. This led to a rejection of any universally valid rational norms for state and society. Later, it was claimed that no bond joins individuals, states, and nations into a whole of mankind, that the particular existential conditions of each cannot be submitted to the general judgement of reason. Laws, it was held, are not based upon any universal qualities of man in whom a reason resides; they rather express the needs of individual people whose lives they regulate in accordance with their existential requirements. This demotion of reason made it possible to exalt certain particularities (such as the race or the folk) to the rank of the highest values.[442]

Assuming the truth of Marcuse's analysis, it does not have application to Stirner. His rejection of universals was radical enough to include Marcuse's "particularities," especially "the race or the folk." The Nazis, in particular, would have had to burn a book containing the following passage:

> The fall of peoples and mankind will invite *me* to my rise.
> Listen, even as I am writing this, the bells begin to sound, that they may jingle in for tomorrow the festival of the thousand years' existence of our dear Germany. Sound, sound its knell! You do sound solemn enough,

---

442 Marcuse, *Reason and Revolution*, p. 267.

as I your tongue was roved by the presentiment that it is giving convoy to a corpse. The German people and German peoples have behind them a history of a thousand years: what a long life! O, go to rest, never to rise again—that all may become free whom you so long have held in fetters—the *people* is dead.—Up with *me*![443]

(Stirner is not, of course, advocating genocide, but the "death" of nationalism.)

Marcuse also characterizes fascism as calling for the sacrifice of the individual:

> The total victimization of the individual that takes place is encouraged for the specific benefit of the industrial and political bureaucracy. It therefore cannot be justified on the ground of the individual's true interest. National Socialist ideology simply states that the true human existence consists in unconditional sacrifice, that it is of the essence of the individual's life to obey and to serve—"service which never comes to an end because service and lie coincide."[444]

It should be unnecessary at this point to adduce any more quotations from Stirner to show his attitude toward self-sacrifice.

It was mentioned above that Carroll, while rejecting Helms's attempt to reveal Stirner as a proto-fascist, was himself sympathetic to the idea of a kinship between Stirner and fascism. He notes a few elements in Stirner's book that, taken out of context, bear a similarity to certain fascist ideas.[445] On the whole, however, he admits that Stirner's "work is categorically anti-authoritarian, that there is no suggestion of racism, and that he had nothing but contempt for German nationalism."[446]He sees Stirner rather

---

443 Stirner, *The Ego and His Own*, p. 217.
444 Marcuse, *Reason and Revolution*, pp. 415-416.
445 Carroll, *Max Stirner: The Ego and His Own*, pp. 168 n.; 170 n.; 193 n.
446 *Ibid.*, p. 16.

as a fascist "by default," in that an apolitical attitude such as that expressed by Stirner opens the way for a seizure of power by the Right.

> The Left, which is committed to political action, and to using efficacious means—large scale organization and violence—has some right to say: "He who is not with us is against us."...In an age of "mass politics", and the centralization of power in the bureaucratic State, the choice to be apolitical is not available...[447]

This contention implies that Stirner's book will be widely read and followed, if only one or two individuals acted on it, they would in any case be unable to stop a seizure of power, whether by Right or by Left. But if Carroll can hypothesize wide-spread acceptance of Stirner's ideas and conclude to a fascist takeover, then it should be legitimate to hypothesize an even more wise-spread acceptance and conclude to an *end* of "mass politics" altogether. Dictatorships require masses of police with unswerving loyalty to their leaders; wars require masses of soldiers imbued with patriotism; political, religious, and racial pogroms require unquestioning belief in a set of abstract principles, along with a tendency to regard other human beings not as unique individuals, but as mere specimens of a hated universal. If Stirner were thoroughly read and correctly understood by all—or most—people, all of these things would become impossible. The danger today is not from the apolitical, but from the political fanatics of both Left and Right.

Stirner will not, of course, be read and understood widely enough to have these large scale effects. But even in the absence of that, he still has his uses: he can give the individual a point of view which will enable him to make his own way in a world dominated by politics.

---

447 *Ibid.*, p. 13.

5. Conclusion: Stirner or Marx?

We have now completed our re-examination of the controversy between Stirner and Marx. It is now time to look back and see what has been accomplished.

The philosophy of Max Stirner offers a possible alternative to those who are attracted to Marxism because of its realistic, naturalistic, and socially radical outlook, but who are repelled by its collectivist view of humanity. Stirner's philosophy grew from the same intellectual soil, at about the same time, and has many features in common with Marxism; but it is radically individualistic.

One obstacle to an acceptance of Stirner's philosophy is the impression that it was refuted, almost at the moment of its birth, by Marx himself. In order to test that impression, we have looked anew at Marx's critique, along with a recent updating of that critique.

Before doing this, we saw that Stirner and Marx offer two options in the same tradition, that of Hegelianism. We saw that the two had accepted many elements from Hegel, including the dialectical method, the conception of history as a progress with successive, well-defined stages, reticence about predicting the future, the close connection between spirit and matter, and the concept of alienation. We also saw that where they differed, this was usually due to selecting different strains of the sometimes ambiguous thought of Heel, as in their different interpretations of universality and individuality. We also saw that their work was based on the reinterpretation of Hegel by the other Young Hegelians; Stirner and Marx extended this reinterpretation in opposite directions.

The controversy between Stirner and Marx turns on the conception of human existence as individual or social, and on the relative importance of ideas in determining conduct. Marx is a collectivist who sees the individual as an organic part of a larger totality; Stirner is a nominalist, for whom only the individual exists, while universals are mental fictions. For Marx, the role of ideas in human conduct is limited to that of mediating the influences of the mode of production; for Stirner, the behavior of the individual is a result of the ideas, true or false, that he has in his mind.

I have tried to show that Marx's criticisms of Stirner were not conclusive, in that many of them were based on a misreading of Stirner's position. I have cited Stirner's own statements, whenever possible, to establish this contention. The same procedure was followed in regard to Helms's interpretation of Stirner as a precursor to fascism: Stirner's position, as expressed in his own words, seems inconsistent with fascist principles on nearly all counts.

At the end of all this, what has been accomplished? Supposing the demonstration that Marx had not refuted Stirner was successful, this by no means constitutes a refutation of Marx; at best, it may have indicated that Stirner's philosophy is worth further examination. Much more work will have to be done in drawing out and examining the implications of Stirner's philosophy before it could pose as a competitor on anything like equal terms with Marxism.

Ultimately, as I suggested at the outset, the choice of a philosophy probably depends more on personal temperament and character than on the validity or truth-value of arguments. The most that can be accomplished, in all probability, is to give those who are attracted to the Marxist type of outlook, but repelled by the specific character of Marxism, an intellectually respectable alternative. This work has been conceived as a very small step in that direction.

Max Stirner Versus Karl Marx

BIBLIOGRAPHY

1. Texts and Translations

A. Hegel

Hegel, Georg Wilhelm Friedrich. *Early Theological Writings*. Trans. T.M. Knox and Richard Kroner. Chicago: The University of Chicago Press, 1948.

_____. *The Phenomenology of Mind*. Trans. with an Introduction and Notes by J.B. Baillie. 2nd ed., revised and corrected. 1931; New York: Humanities Press, 1964.

_____. *The Philosophy of History*. Trans. J. Sibree, with Prefaces by Charles Hegel and the Translator, and a new Introduction by C.J. Friedrich. New York: Dover Publications, 1956.

_____. *Werke in zwanzig Bänden*. Frankfurt am Main: Suhrkamp Verlag, 1971.

Johnston, W.H. and Struthers, L.G. (trans.). *Hegel's Science of Logic*. 2 Vols. 1929; London: George Allen & Unwin; New York: The Macmillan Company, 1951.

Knox, T.M. (trans.). *Hegel's Philosophy of Right*. 1952; London, Oxford, and New York: Oxford University Press, 1969.

_____. *Hegel's Political Writings*. With an Introductory Essay by Z.A. Pelczynski. Oxford: At the Clarendon Press, 1964.

Loewenberg, Jacob (ed.). *Hegel: Selections*. New York: Charles Scribner's Sons, 1929.

Mueller, Gustav Emil (trans.). *Hegel: Encyclopedia of Philosophy*. New York: Philosophical Library, 1959.

B. Marx and Engels

Easton, Loyd D., and Guddat, Kurt H. (eds. and trans.). *Writings of the Young Marx on Philosophy and Society*. Garden City, N.Y.: Doubleday & Company, 1967.

Feuer, Lewis S. (ed.). *Marx and Engels: Basic Writings on Politics and Philosophy*. Garden City, N.Y.: Doubleday & Company, 1959.

Marx, Karl. *Capital: A Critique of Political Economy*. Ed. Friedrich Engels. Vol. I: *The Process of Capitalist Production*. Trans. S. Moore and Edward Aveling. Chicago: Charles H. Kerr & Company, 1909.

Vol. II: *The Process of Circulation of Capital*. Trans. Ernest Untermann. Chicago: Charles H. Kerr & Company, 1907.

Vol. III: *The Process of Capitalist Production as a Whole*. Trans. Ernest Untermann. Chicago: Charles H. Kerr & Company, 1909.

Marx, Karl, and Engels, Frederick. *The German Ideology*. Translated from the German. Ed. S. Ryazanskaya. London: Lawrence & Wishart, 1965.

_____. *Selected Works*. 2 Vols. London: Lawrence & Wishart, 1950.

Marx, Karl, and Engels, Friedrich. *Werke*. 38+II Vols. Berlin: Dietz Verlag, 1961-71.

C. Stirner

Carroll, John (ed.). *Max Stirner: The Ego and His Own*. "Roots of the Right: Readings in Fascist Racist and Elitist Ideology." General ed.: George Steiner. London: Jonathan Cape, 1971.

Mackay, John Henry (ed.). *Max Stirners kleinere Schriften und seine Entgegnungen auf die Kritik seines Werkes: "Der Einzige und sein Eigenthum." Aus den Jahren 1842-1847*. Berlin: Schuster & Loeffler, 1898.

Stirner, Max (Johann Kaspar Schmidt). *Der Einzige und sein Eigenthum*. Leipzig: Otto Wigand, 1845.

_____. *The Ego and His Own: The Case of the Individual Against Authority*, trans. Steven T. Byington; ed., with annotations and an introduction, by James J. Martin. New York: Libertarian Book Club, 1963.

_____. *The False Principle of Our Education, or Humanism and Realism*, trans. Robert H. Beebe; ed. with annotation and an introduction by James J. Martin. Colorado Springs, Colorado: Ralph Miles, 1967.

2. Books

Althusser, Louis. *For Marx*, trans. Ben Brewster. New York: Random House, 1970.

Arvon, Henri. *Aux sources de l'existentialisme: Max Stirner*. Paris: Presses Universitaires de France, 1954

Avineri, Shlomo. *The Social and Political of Karl Marx*. Cambridge: At the University Press, 1968.

Bober, M.M. *Marx's Interpretation of History*. 2nd ed., revised; New York: W. W. Norton & Company, 1965.

Burnham, James. *The Managerial Revolution*. 1941; Bloomington: Indiana University Press, 1962.

Dupré, Louis. *The Philosophical Foundations of Marxism*. New York: Harcourt, Brace & World, 1966.

Edwards, Paul (ed.). *The Encyclopedia of Philosophy*. 8 Vols. New York: The Macmillan Company and The Free Press, 1967.

Feuer, Lewis S. *Marx and the Intellectuals: A Set of Post-Ideological Essays*. Garden City, N.Y.: Doubleday & Company, 1969.

Feuerbach, Ludwig. *The Essence of Christianity*, trans. from the 2nd German ed. by Marian Evans. New York: C. Blanchard, 1955.

Findlay, J. N. *Hegel: A Re-examination*. 1958; New York: Collier Books, 1962.

Foster, Michael Beresford. *The Political Philosophies of Plato and Hegel*. 1935; New York: Russell & Russell, 1965.

Fromm, Erich. *Marx's Concept of Man*. New York: Frederick Ungar Publishing Company, 1967.

Helms, Hans G. *Die Ideologie der anonymen Gesellschaft: Max Stirners >Einziger< und der Fortschritt des demokratischen Selbstbewusstseins vom Vormarz biz zur Bundesrepublik.*

Köln: Verlag M. Du Mont Schauberg, 1966.

Hook, Sidney. *From Hegel to Marx: Studies in the Intellectual Development of Karl Marx.* 1936; Ann Arbor: The University of Michigan Press, 1968.

Huneker, James. *Egoists: A Book of Supermen.* 1909; New York; Charles Scribner's Sons, 1932.

Kaufmann, Walter (ed.). *Hegel's Political Philosophy.* New York: Atherton Press, 1970.

_____. *Hegel: Reinterpretation, Texts, and Commentary.* Garden City, N.Y.: Doubleday & Company, 1965.

Löwith, Karl. *From Hegel to Nietzsche: The Revolution in Nineteenth-Century Thought,* trans. David E. Green. 1941; Garden City, N. Y.: Doubleday & Company, 1967.

Mackay, John Henry. *Max Stirner: Sein Leben und sein Werk.* Berlin: Verlag von Schuster & Loeffler, 1898.

Marcuse, Herbert. *Reason and Revolution: Hegel and the Rise of Social Theory.* 2nd ed.; New York: Humanities Press, 1954.

McLellan, David. *The Thought of Karl Marx: An Introduction.* London: Macmillan, 1971.

_____. *The Young Hegelians and Karl Marx.* New York and Washington: Frederick A. Praeger, 1969.

McTaggart, J. M . E . *Studies in the Hegelian Dialectic.* New York: Cambridge University Press, 1896.

Mehring, Franz. *Karl Marx: The Story of His Life* trans. Edward Fitzgerald; ed. Ruth and Heinz

Norden . New York: Covici, Friede, 1935.

Milton C. Nahm, *Selections from Early Greek Philosophy.* 4th ed.; New York: Appleton-Century-Crofts, 1964.

Paterson, R.W.K. *The Nihilistic Egoist: Max Stirner.* London and New York: Oxford University Press, 1971.

Plechanoff, George. *Anarchism and Socialism,* trans. Eleanor Marx Aveling. Chicago: Charles H. Kerr & Company, 1909.

Pelczynski, Z. A. (ed.). *Hegel's Political Philosophy: Problems and Perspectives.* Cambridge: At the University Press, 1971.

Popper, Karl R. *The Open Society and its Enemies*, Vol. II: *The High Tide of Prophecy: Hegel,*
Marx, and the Aftermath. 5th ed., revised; London: Routledge and Kegan Paul, 1966.

Read, Herbert. *The Tenth Muse: Essays in Criticism*. London: Routledge and Kegan Paul, 1957.

Rosenberg, Alfred. *Der Mythus des 20. Jahrhunderts*. München: Hoheneichen-Verlag, 1939.

Stace, W . T. *The Philosophy of Hegel*. 1924 ; New York: Dover, 1955.

Strauss, David Friedrich. *The Life of Jesus*, trans. From the 4th German ed. by George Eliot. 4th ed.; London: S. Sonnenschein, 1902.

Taylor, Frederick W. *The Principles of Scientific Management*. New York: Harper & Brothers, 1911.

Tucker, Robert C. *Philosophy and Myth in Karl Marx*. Cambridge: At the University Press, 1969.

Whitehead, Alfred North. *Process and Reality: An Essay in Cosmology*. 1929; New York: Harper & Row, 1960.

Wolfson, Harry Austryn. *The Philosophy of Spinoza*. 1934; 2 Vols. in one; New York: The World Publishing Company, 1965.

Woodcock, George. *Anarchism: A History of Libertarian Ideas and Movements*. Cleveland and New York: The World Publishing Company, 1962

3. Articles

Bergmann, Frithjof. "The Purpose of Hegel's System," *Journal of the History of Philosophy*, Vol. II, No. 2 (1964), 202-208.

Mueller, Gustav Emil. "The Hegel Legend of Thesis-Antithesis-Synthesis," *Journal of the History of Ideas*, Vol. XIX, No. 3 (June 1958), 411-414.

Zube, Kurt. Review of *Die Ideologie der anonymen Gesellschaft*, Erlesenes, No. 1 (1967 68), 61-62.

Max Stirner Versus Karl Marx

www.ingramcontent.com/pod-product-compliance
Lightning Source LLC
Chambersburg PA
CBHW052001090426
42741CB00008B/1503